Negotiating a skree trail on Kachess Ridge

kissing the Trail

greater seattle mountain bicycle adventures

John Zilly

Adventure Press
Seattle • Ketchum

Adventure Press
P.O. Box 14059
Seattle, Washington 98114

Copyediting: Ella M. David
Maps: John Zilly

Cover: An A.H. Waite photo, circa 1900, of the photographer's bicycle near Longmire, on the southwest slope of Mount Rainier (courtesy of Special Collections Division, University of Washington Libraries, A.H. Waite #305-15)
Inset photo: Wade Praeger

Library of Congress Catalog Card Number: 93-70778
John Zilly
Kissing the Trail: Greater Seattle Mountain Bicycle Adventures

ISBN 1-881583-03-1

ACKNOWLEDGMENTS

Steve Hall was the catalyst to get this project rolling; his assistance kept the project focused. His ideas always proved useful. It's difficult to imagine this book without his help.

M. Angela Castañeda helped me tremendously on *Kissing the Trail* with ideas, assistance, and constant encouragement. And despite the stresses of bookwriting, I fell in love with her while I wrote it. She is my first-kiss experience.

For their assistance and contributions, thanks to Ruth Flanders, Scott Larson, Nancy Penrose, Donald Marcy, Mike Clyde, John Ensinck, Mark Klebanoff, Mary Anne Christy, Fred Wilson, and Lisa Dally Wilson.

And for all the standing around in the rain while I stared at the map, thanks to my riding partners Wade Praeger, Greg Strong, and especially my brother Peter Zilly who helped me more than he can imagine.

OVERVIEW MAP

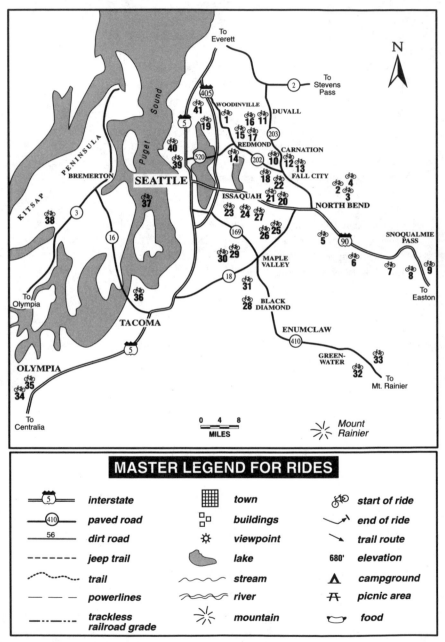

N

To
Everett

To
Stevens
Pass

2

405

WOODINVILLE
1

DUVALL

16 11

5

41

19

15 17

REDMOND

CARNATION

203

40

520

14

202

10

12 13

FALL CITY

39

SEATTLE

18

22

4

BREMERTON

37

ISSAQUAH

21 20

2

3

PENINSULA

23 24 27

NORTH BEND

KITSAP

38

3

169

26 25

5

90

SNOQUALMIE
PASS

16

30 29

6

7   8   9

18

MAPLE
VALLEY

To
Easton

To
Olympia

36

31

BLACK
DIAMOND

28

TACOMA

ENUMCLAW

410

OLYMPIA

5

GREEN-
WATER

33

32

34 35

To
Mt. Rainier

To
Centralia

0   4   8
MILES

Mount
Rainier

MASTER LEGEND FOR RIDES

══5══	*interstate*	▦	*town*	🚲	*start of ride*
─410─	*paved road*	▫▫	*buildings*	↘	*end of ride*
─56─	*dirt road*	☼	*viewpoint*	↘	*trail route*
-------	*jeep trail*	▨	*lake*	680'	*elevation*
••••••	*trail*	∿	*stream*	▲	*campground*
─ ─ ─	*powerlines*	≈	*river*	🕇	*picnic area*
─··─··─	*trackless railroad grade*	☼	*mountain*	⌣	*food*

CONTENTS

RIDES BY DIFFICULTY

BE RESPONSIBLE FOR YOURSELF

The author and publisher of *Kissing the Trail* disclaim and are in no way responsible or liable for the consequences of using this guide.

1. *Mountain biking is dangerous.* Cyclists can get lost, become injured, or suffer from serious fatigue. The difficulty of the trails described in this guide and the level of skill and experience required to ride safely on the trails are subjective. It is incumbent on each rider to assess his or her preparedness for a trail in light of his or her own skills, experience, and equipment.

2. *Trail conditions are subject to change without notice.* The information contained in this book, as of the date of publication, was as accurate as possible. But conditions on these routes change quickly: storms, logging, stream revisions, land slides, trail construction, and development, among other things, drastically alter the landscape and its trails, in some cases making the trails dangerous and/or unridable.

3. *Do not ride on any private property unless you are sure the landowner has granted permission.* Many of the rides described in this guide either cross or are entirely within private land. Do not conclude that the owner has granted you permission to use the trails listed in this book. Some land owners post signs that allow nonintrusive, daytime use by bicyclists and other users. If the property is not signed, and you are not sure of its status, you should obtain permission from the owner before riding on the property.

4. *Public jurisdictions may change rules at any time.* Most of the rides described in this guide are located on public land. Although these are currently legal rides, in the future land managers may exclude bicycles, regulate bicycle use, or require permits. Understanding the laws as they change is up to you.

The author assumes absolutely no responsibility for these or any other problems that may occur, nor should he. Hey kids, be responsible for yourselves and the land you are using: Keep the rubber side down, pay attention, bring a wool hat and lots of date bars, and be cool to the earth.

NOTE: In January 1993 a severe windstorm hit the Puget Sound area. Many of the trails in the area have been affected by fallen trees. Although much of this blowdown will be cleared at some time in the future, be aware that you will have to carry your bike over or around many of these obstacles until they are moved.

Freelancing after a storm

BE COOL TO THE EARTH

Controversy swirls around many guide books: revealing this wonderful place to the masses will surely ruin it. To someone who loves the solitude and majesty of special places, it is certainly a dilemma. Why would I want more people out on the trails I love? Why would I want more people intruding into my peace, diminishing my experience? Why tell more people about these great adventures?

This don't-tell-anyone attitude represents short-range thinking. I want to hike the Pacific Crest Trail at age seventy. But when I asked a friend to plan on the trip, some forty years in the future, he said, "There won't be a Pacific Crest Trail when we're seventy." He could be right: economic and social pressures have greatly reduced the miles of trails in this country over the past twenty years.

Yet to preserve trails and primitive areas—especially those close to urban centers—more people, not fewer, need to know and love them. When more people have experienced the trails in a particular area, then we'll have more voices to shout when development or logging or governmental cutbacks or other user groups threaten to eliminate that area. I am a conservationist, committed to preserving the public lands we all own. But most folks don't appreciate the public lands until they have spent some time in them, felt their beauty and power and magnificence. It's true, sending people out to trails in primitive areas causes greater impact on those places, but it's also true that more people will learn to love the land, land that shouldn't be mined or clearcut, land that the Forest Service should keep their road-building machinery away from, land that saves the world's diversity, helps us breathe and clear out our minds. We must either use the land or lose it.

But not only am I a conservationist concerned with getting people out on the trails, I'm also a conservationist who rides a mountain bicycle. Unfortunately, due to a few renegade bikers, mountain bicyclists have a rather bad reputation vis-à-vis the environment, a reputation we don't deserve. Due to this bad reputation, 60 percent of the trails in Washington State have been closed to mountain bikes. This short-sighted action by other user groups and trail bureaucrats will actually decrease and degrade the number of trails and primitive areas rather than increase and enhance them. That's because these groups are spurning a huge pool of conservationists—mountain bicyclists—who also want to preserve, and indeed, increase the number of primitive areas. Bicycles and bicyclists have always been part of the conservation movement, and mountain bikes are no different. Mountain bicyclists don't demand paved trails, which are expensive and degrade the land's beauty. Mountain bicyclists usually don't camp overnight on the land that they use, cutting down on that serious impact. Mountain bicyclists can often ride to the trailhead, thus cars are driven less and there's no need for parking lots that encroach on already-limited public land. And mountain bicyclists are generally cycling enthusiasts, commuting to work, riding to the store, and pedaling rather than pulling out the car for a Sunday drive.

If all goes well, if we pedal into primitive areas to enjoy the land and also help preserve it, perhaps I'll be able to hike the Pacific Crest Trail in the year 2030 after all.

THE FIRST KISS

When was your first kiss? Steady yourself and think back for a moment. My first kiss took place one summer afternoon on top of a dog house. It had been planned for several days; the locale was carefully chosen for its secluded nature, although in retrospect the choice seems more like a podium than a secret kissing alcove. Since the dog house was taller than either of us, Tina and I helped each other climb to the crest. Moments later the first kiss ensued. Bliss. The kissman, kiss-o-rama, kisselodeon, osculating on the dog house, winning the Oscar, making a speech, kisstosterone, kiss-o-mania, k-i-s-s. Since then the moment has tirelessly wandered the back alleys of my memory, exposing itself to my consciousness every so often, as if to say, "Don't be so serious, or safe, or sure of the way things should proceed." Shouldn't there be more moments like this that flow through your mind's hot-water pipes, radiating energy? When is the next event that will resonate with first-kiss magnitude?

Pump up the tires and hold on tight. For this, trust one Neil Cassidy, an infamous iconoclast of the Beat Generation and beyond, friend of Kerouac, Kesey, and The Grateful Dead. Cassidy lived a fervid, shortish life, driving cartwheel colored buses, borrowed cars, and possibly owned Cadillacs all over the Americas, always searching. The nectar is in the journey! In a song about Neil Cassidy, John Barlow writes, "Ah, child of boundless trees. Ah, child of boundless seas. What you are, what you're meant to be . . . " And later, Cassidy is "lost now on these country miles in his Cadillac." Whenever I hear these lines, I have strong urges to unpack my child of boundless dreams and hit the road.

This doesn't necessarily mean that we all ought to file into the boss's office and quit; it means we need to get a grip on reality. Over the past twenty years, Americans have dispensed with about half of their free time. Between commuting, longer work hours, multi-career families, we don't have much free time left. The average person (car, job, kid, and basement that resembles a landfill) has just sixteen hours of free time a week after brushing his teeth and shoveling in that microwaved entrée. It has become a monumental task to scrounge enough time for a weekend outing, let alone a drive across America. But we can use the time we do have in a passionate and adventurous manner, rather than a tepid and guarded one. That's why mountain bikers are becoming the hikers of the nineties. In less time, mountain bicyclists can get a workout and a primitive, backcountry experience, and still make it home in time to pick up the kid from painting class. *Kissing the Trail* provides forty-one great mountain bike trails for all abilities, all within an hour's drive of Seattle. No other mountain bike guide book locates so many rides so close to home on good, soft-surface, public *and* private trails. Charging out to experience life with the passion of that first kiss is still possible.

Kissing the Trail is about mountain biking with an attitude, of holding on to boundless dreams, of mediating the stresses of the nineties, but it's also about being safe and considerate and conservation-minded while out on the trail. It is possible to have a serious craving for a first-kiss experience and still pay attention to where you are and how you got there, to care for the few giant cedars left in the forest, and to be courteous to others using the same trail. More preaching, prophesying, and playing to come, so open an unknown door, skip off to see the wizard, cop a lost-now-on-a-country-road-in-a-Cadillac feel (even if the p.c. rating of a Caddy is, well, tank empty).

USING THIS GUIDE

Whether you began mountain biking yesterday or have been racing for years, this trail guide is exactly what you need to explore the trails around Puget Sound. Despite the setback of numerous trail closures, hundreds of miles of excellent public and private "community" trails still exist in the Puget Sound region. *Kissing the Trail* is simple to use. The straightforward format makes it easy to find and digest the information you want. In addition, even if two rides begin from the same trailhead, they are treated as two separate rides, so the confusing exercise of skipping every other paragraph is eliminated. Here's a rundown of the information provided with each ride.

Difficulty rating

The difficulty rating of each ride is measured from **1 to 5 wheels**, depending on the length of the trip, the hill factor, and the level of riding skill needed to complete the ride. This quick, although subjective, reference is located at the top of each ride.

Easy: Just about anyone can ride a one-wheel ride; it isn't much different from riding on a paved country road. These rides are generally short, not very hilly, and have a well-packed riding surface. One-wheel rides stick to wide, nontechnical dirt roads.

Intermediate: A two-wheel ride also traverses primarily dirt roads, but it can wander onto jeep roads and trails. These rides are longer and have more elevation gain than one-wheelers. Although the riding isn't very technical, some riders may have to walk short sections or dismount to cross obstacles.

Difficult: During a three-wheel ride you may encounter dirt roads, and you will definitely experience some narrow, single-track trails. These rides are longer, have some steep climbs, and cross tricky spots in the trail which will likely require walking your bike, perhaps over some longer sections.

Most Difficult: If a ride is long, has lots of hills, and is full of technical riding, I have rated it four wheels. Some riders may have to push and carry their bikes for long stretches during these rides. This is fun: if you're not hiking, you're not mountain biking.

Extreme: Two rides were sufficiently difficult to warrant an expert, five-wheel rating. These rides are long, extremely technical, and dangerous. Do not attempt these rides unless you are an expert mountain bicyclist and in excellent physical condition. But these rides are incredibly beautiful alpine experiences, and, despite the dangers, worth the effort.

Ride statistics

Checklist Trip distance and riding surface are noted at the top of each ride. Remember that each mile ridden in the mountains equals three to five miles of riding on the road. Each ride is labeled either **Out & Back**, **Loop**, or **One Way**. One Way means that the ride doesn't finish at the same place it began.

Duration The duration of each ride is listed, although with some reservation since this is perhaps the most subjective of all ratings. The duration of a ride in Capitol Forest, for example, could vary from an hour and a half to seven hours, depending on the rider.

Hill factor Every rider wants to know what the hills are like on a certain ride. The hill factor describes the difficulty of the hills. The elevation marked on each map identifies the high point of that ride; the starting elevation is also included. I have noted many of the major climbs in the ride description. Many of the rides traverse hilly terrain, changing quickly from climbing to descending. Most riders will have to walk during some section of each ride.

Skill level Rides are rated **beginner**, **intermediate**, **advanced**, or **expert** depending on the amount of riding skill needed. Skill level rates the minimum bicycle handling abilities a rider should have before attempting a particular trail. It has nothing to do with fitness.

Season This is the best time of year to be out on this trail.

Maps Maps are mandatory, unless you enjoy bivouacking with your bicycle. I've listed the best map for each ride, usually a United States Geological Survey map (USGS) or a Green Trails Map. Often a park's own map proves extremely helpful.

Ownership I have listed the ownership of the land for each trail—**public** or **private**. However, be aware that ownership, or the rules an owner uses, can change overnight.

User density The volume of other trail users is listed—**low**, **medium**, **high**—depending on how many other bikers, equestrians, pedestrians, or other users you are likely to find. I have listed which types of users you are likely to encounter. The presence of other users means it's a beautiful, multi-use trail, not that there will be user conflict.

Hazards Any hazards that I noticed while researching *Kissing the Trail* are mentioned. I survived. Use your own judgment.

Prelude

Each ride begins with a paragraph that presents a subjective sense of the ride. Magic is performed in these few sentences, images form, and ride karma is released.

To get there

Locating the starting point of each ride is simple—just read the "To get there" section for concise directions to each trailhead. The small bike on each map  marks the beginning of the ride. More map information can be found on the Overview Map and the Master Legend for Rides opposite the table of contents.

The ride

The primary reason to have this book in hand is to find the trail and then stay on it. The Ride section contains a detailed description of the terrain—up or down, left or right. These paragraphs note the mileage for most forks in the trail, hills, and other significant landmarks. The arrows on each map point out the bike route; the arrow with a line denotes the end of the ride. Mileages are in bold; watch for the word "**Whoa**" which signifies a tricky or dangerous section of trail. If you're hungry for more, some rides have additional riding suggestions (**Additions**) beneath the Ride section, so go explore.

Mountain bicycling involves a lot more than finding the trailhead and knowing when to turn left. So I have also included sections on safety, riding techniques, repairs, how to avoid getting lost, training, maintenance, land issues, and ethics.

Here are my goals for this book: To inform families, weekend cyclists, and mountain-bike fanatics about great trails; to get them to ride in a safe and intelligent way; to spread out mountain bicyclists onto lots of trails; to show that users can share trails without conflict; and to re-teach people something they already know—that bicyclists really are part of the conservation movement.

Crossing a creek on Tiger Mountain. Each ride requires different skill and stamina levels: choose each ride carefully.

SAFETY

I felt a tremendous rush the first time I rode a bicycle without training wheels at age seven, like the stomach-beat during a roller coaster's first descent. Part of the excitement of riding a bicycle for the first time was the realization that I had discovered something very dangerous. It never quite made sense to me that my parents encouraged me to go riding as much as they did. "If you go near that construction site, you'll be grounded for a month! Why don't you go out and ride your bike instead." Okay, I'm not supposed to dig in the dirt around an unfinished building, but riding around the neighborhood is perfectly safe? I don't think so. Although it wouldn't get me in trouble, riding straight down dirt embankments, sailing off plywood jumps, trying to avoid stray vehicles, vicious dogs, and neighborhood bullies was certainly unsafe.

I still get wide-eyed on certain sections of trail: riding a bike through the mountains can be a dangerous undertaking. It's best to avoid crashing altogether by riding at moderate speeds in a controlled manner, and staying away from trails above your ability. Of course, if you ride long enough, a fall is inevitable. To minimize the effects of a bad crash, always wear a helmet, carry a first-aid kit, and ride with a friend. If, after the crash, you are unable to move, your friend can help you into your extra clothes to prevent shock, prop some water and food next to you, then scurry off for help.

But the danger of mountain biking isn't just the big crash. A simple mechanical failure, a sore knee, or exhaustion can strand you miles from the trailhead and force an unplanned night in the woods. If you don't have the proper supplies like some food, extra clothes, plenty of water, a light, and a stick to fend off the wild pigs, you are in trouble; the adventure has rusted through. Everyone defines danger and adventure differently: Turn around before your adventure turns into a nightmare.

Minimize the risk

- Never ride alone.
- Always wear a helmet. Helmets protect against over 75 percent of all head and neck injuries that would occur without a helmet.
- Avoid violent speed experiences and out-of-control riding. Watch out for other trail users, ruts, roots, rocks, fallen trees, cliffs, and all animals.
- Carry a good first-aid kit and know how to use it. Also toss sunscreen, a lighter, and a pocket knife into that fanny pack.
- Wear some eye protection.
- Take two quarts of water per person per day. Don't count on finding water.
- Always, always, always take along a good map. Ask about the area before you leave, and take this book. A compass and an odometer won't hurt, either. Don't try playing *Journey to the Center of the Earth*.
- Carry extra clothes (hat, gloves, jacket, long underwear, wind pants) no matter how nice the weather seems, some food, and a flashlight.
- Make sure someone in the group has the proper bike-repair tools.
- Is it hunting season? Wear a bell and something bright, or go road riding. A bullet hole in your new jersey is a sure way to ruin the ride.

VIRTUOUS MOUNTAIN CYCLING

You're out on the trail, admiring an enormous cedar, listening to the river below, rolling down a quick hill. You're having quite a bit more fun than you do at work, at least a thousand times the fun. This is not, however, the time to disconnect your intuition about good and bad; it's time to listen to your heart and ask, "How do I go out into a primitive area on a bike and act virtuously? What's the point of being out here anyway?"

Well, there needs to be magic and wonder. Stop to watch a deer in the meadow, a hawk, a small, spirited stream empowered with snow melt; see a chipmunk chipmunking instead of a co-worker bitching; discover the smell of a pine forest instead of the electrified-defrosted-conditioned-reconstituted-smogged-exhausted air of the city.

It's true, there is a roller-coaster element to mountain biking. The adventure involves speed, technical riding skills, a modicum of danger, and buckets of physicality. But adventure alone will get old if you don't have the romance along with it, the magic. If you are not after this magic, if all that interests you is raging down one hill after another, stay home and turn on the television; you are not wanted on the trail.

Fortunately, the speed freaks and havoc wreakers represent a small minority of the mountain bike community, just as hikers who cheat by cutting switchbacks are a minority in that community. Most riders do search out the magic that's hidden around each bend in the trail. These are the ones who always yield the trail to others and help maintain trails. And this group of virtuous riders is growing so rapidly, it's clear that mountain bikers will be the hikers of the nineties.

But it's not quite that easy. Mountain bicyclists have been made pariahs of the forest, banned here, restricted there. What follows is a discussion of the issues, and non-issues, that have brought mountain bicyclists to this point.

Riders sharing the Lake Washington Bicycle Path, circa 1900

Safely

Earlier, I explained that mountain bikers can be terrors to themselves—flying off cliffs, bobbing down streams, launching into large trees. Now, discussing ethics, I need to explain the concept of public safety. Only your mom cares if you fly off the edge of a canyon, but when you careen around a corner and run down small children, many people care. But it's not about who cares; the virtuous rider wouldn't run anyone down.

The safety problem arises because mountain bikers are quiet and can sometimes travel more quickly than pedestrians. On downhills, cyclists can

Mountain bicycle pioneers near Lake Washington, circa 1900

come up on other users quickly. To alleviate a mishap, ride as if a small child is around every corner. On long downhill sections, attach a bell to your bike so you sound like a cow to other trail users. All trail users simply need to be considerate of each other. If you are out on the trail, yield to all trail users, whether hikers, equestrians, motorcyclists, or other bicyclists.

The United States Forest Service has banned mountain bicycles from many trails. Close to Seattle, for instance, the North Bend Ranger District permits mountain bicycles on just three short trails, only one of which is really ridable. Signs are posted pronouncing the trail closed due to user conflict. Since I haven't seen users fist-fighting, I assume the rangers are concerned about the safety of the different types of users on the same trail. I mountain biked several thousand miles during the research for *Kissing the Trail*, and I never had a conflict with another trail user. Moreover, I never had a conflict while researching *The Mountain Bike Adventure Guide* or the *Son of the Mountain Bike Adventure Guide*, two guide books I wrote for central Idaho. Indeed, cars, trucks, bicycles, and pedestrians share roadways all over the world and we're not about to ban any one of those groups from the streets; even forks and spoons manage to share the small quarters of the plate without conflict. The point here is that just because the uses are different does not mean they are incompatible. Bicyclists have been sharing soft-surface trails around Puget Sound for over one hundred years.

The environment

Everyone who enters a primitive area must take responsibility to minimize his or her impact. Although "no trace use" is the code of the day, all travelers impact the environment—even if it's a turned pine cone or a lingering odor. An average mountain bike weighs about 30 pounds, less than a full backpack, so a loaded hiker bounding down the trail weighs more than a mountain bicyclist (equestrians are off the scale). True, trail damage based on weight doesn't tell the entire tale, but on dry, well-built trails, Vibram-footed hikers and rolling wheels have about the same impact. On poorly constructed trails and on all trails during bad weather, all users cause damage. It's up to each user—pedestrian, equestrian, cyclist—to survey the impact and then take steps to prevent damage, perhaps by even turning around.

Some areas are susceptible to damage; in other areas, four-wheel drives, backhoes, and similar motorized machines have created roads or sometimes mud pits where winding trails had been. Some of the trails described in *Kissing the Trail* follow six-foot-wide muddy trails. Go ahead and get muddy on these. But most of the trails included here deserve much more care. Observe the trail carefully, use good sense to determine whether it ought to be ridden.

There is one specific type of damage that mountain bikes do have an exclusive claim to—tire impressions. These are created by the skidding action of beginning cyclists. Mountain bikers should learn how to ride to prevent skidding (unless on pavement or gravel). Simply riding on a particularly delicate trail can cause damage—a slight dent can form which might cause erosion during a hard rain. To prevent this, always watch the trail for signs of damage. Trail conditions can change quickly, so one section of a ride might be fine while the next section should not be used. Turn around if you are causing damage. In addition, the virtuous rider picks up litter and removes obstacles from the trail. If every trail user spent a few minutes picking up litter as well as clearing and otherwise maintaining the trails, the difference would be tremendous.

The greatest damage to trails and the environment comes not from wheels or boots but simply from overuse. The Alpine Lakes Wilderness, near Snoqualmie Pass, has been heavily damaged by the million hikers and equestrians each year who enter its boundaries. Similarly, sections of trail in the Redmond Watershed are damaged because so many mountain bikers use the area. The key is to act virtuously *and* spread out the use. Over the past twenty years, the number of miles of trails in the United States has actually decreased while the population has continued its steady climb: more people are traversing each trail. There is a need for more trails—on primitive and semi-primitive land close to urban areas—that are open to all users. Open trail policies combined with maps and other resources like *Kissing the Trail* will help disperse trail use, and thus minimize the most serious environmental impact—overcrowding.

Aesthetics

Hiking groups have been exceptionally vocal in their opposition to mountain bikes. But it's an aesthetic problem, not a trail-use problem: user conflict and environmental damage are euphemisms for a not-on-my-trail attitude held by a few flannel-shirted bullies. Of course, these dull, mingy-minded thinkers have been around for a long time. In an 1882 article for *The Wheelman* about mountain biking in the Rocky Mountains, the writer and bicyclist W.O. Owen wrote that he met a "big, burly fellow" in La Porte, Colorado, who called Owen's bicycle "some infernal machine, or Yankee contrivance."

Mountain bicycles have offended such hikers' sensibilities. They hiked in to the lake, camped, and don't want to see any foam-helmeted cyclist roll up at 10 a.m. I understand. However, it's not the bike or the helmet that's the problem, it's the feeling that another person is infringing on your space. When I go mountain biking, I don't want to see a zillion people. If I do, I'll select a different trail the next time. And if I spend five hours hiking up to a secluded lake, I'm disappointed if confronted with a set of yellow, domed tents. Most trail users venture into primitive areas to get away from the crowds, to be self-sufficient, to be out there, not to be accosted by other humans. Indeed, the sight of unprepared trail users panhandling for water and granola bars on a hot day isn't why we head out into the woods.

Some have argued, spuriously of course, that mountain bicycles are a new use, and thus upset the proprietary grip hikers and equestrians hold on public lands; others just say mountain bicyclists are environmentally bankrupt. But while the term "mountain bicycle" is relatively new, hearty cyclists have been experiencing the beauty and wonder of remote areas on bicycles for over a century. In an article describing a bicycle tour from Laramie to Cheyenne, Wyoming, in an 1883 issue of *The Wheelman*, W.O. Owen writes: "All around us beautiful evergreens tossed in the wind, each one gorgeously attired in Nature's own drapery; frost sparkling brilliantly in the sun's rays and dazing the eye with its silvery scintillation." Owen was out there for the same reason most mountain bikers are—for the wonderful experience of biking through Nature.

The dispute over rights

Despite the reasonable nature of mountain bikers, many areas have been closed to us. The problem? The dispute over rights. Currently, mountain bikes are excluded from trails in all national parks and completely barred from all designated wilderness areas. In addition, many local jurisdictions have restricted the use of mountain bikes. Around Puget Sound, bicycles are banned on trails in Mount Rainier National Park, the Alpine Lakes Wilderness, many trails in the Snoqualmie–Mount Baker National Forest, the Pacific Crest Trail, most of Cougar Mountain, much of Tiger Mountain and Squak Mountain, and in Seattle city parks.

Mountain bicycles are banned even though thousands of miles of trails exist where bicycles would be perfectly suited. For instance, Cougar and Tiger mountains, two large, semi-primitive mountains in the Issaquah

A motorcycle rut in Tahuya State Forest

A *ride through Nature*

Alps, were almost completely denuded early this century. Many miles of old railroad grades, forgotten utility roads, and abandoned logging roads, hidden by second-growth forests, crisscross the two mountains. Pedestrians use some of these routes frequently, others rarely, if at all, yet mountain bikes are restricted. Why?

As far as I can tell, the restrictions originated from a semantic problem: during the recent mountain bicycle boom, land managers didn't have a column in their manuals for mountain bicycles. Egged on by a small number of belligerent hikers, the managers penned in mountain bikes next to motorcycles. But bicycles are fundamentally different from motorcycles; when motors hit mud, noise explodes through the forest, exhaust boils up around the flora, and pieces of trail splatter in all directions. The virtuous mountain biker tiptoes across delicate areas; I've never seen a motorcyclist sling the machine over his shoulder and tiptoe anywhere.

To make matters worse, grandfather rights have allowed the continued access of horses and miners, both egregious environmental offenders, into Wilderness areas— the most pristine lands we have. Miners cause more damage on public lands than all other users combined. They build roads up unstable hillsides, dig huge holes in the earth, throw dangerous tailings all over the place, and drag in all manner of equipment to help them. Horses, nearly as bad, dig up the flora, stomp right through delicate spots, and sometimes eradicate hillside trails. Low-impact adventuring dictates that you bury your pucky 100 yards from any water and pack out the used paper; horses are allowed to deposit bushel loads in the middle of the trail. Give me a break.

What's the deal with grandfather rights anyway? The city of Seattle recently installed a stop sign at the end of the street I have lived on for ten years. Do I have the grandfather right to ignore that stop sign? I don't think so.

All users need to make a personal decision about the way they interact with the woods. If the way you interact with public land adversely affects me, then either you shouldn't be doing it, or you should pay me for the inconvenience. When trail users damage sensitive areas—and there can be no argument that motorcyclists, equestrians, and miners do—they should pay the rest of us for damaging our land (through restrictions and taxes based on the impact). You can help educate land managers, legislators, and the media about mountain bicycling (see page 33). Tell them which trails you enjoy, which closed trails you would like to enjoy, and then tell them you are a bicyclist *and* an environmentalist. It's not an oxymoron.

Green mountain biking

Cyclists have been a central part of the conservation movement for years—commuting, vacationing, running errands on bicycles. Hearty cyclists have been adventuring into semi-primitive and primitive areas around Seattle since the Great Seattle Fire in 1889. Here are some of the ways in which today's mountain bicyclists have continued this tradition of "green" living. **1.** Mountain bicycles spread out trail use so that each area receives less impact. **2.** Mountain biking motivates more people to get out to areas that should be preserved. **3.** Mountain bicyclists generally don't spend the night in the woods, eliminating that impact. **4.** Mountain bicyclists can often pedal to the trailhead instead of driving, cutting the need for paved parking areas. **5.** Mountain bicyclists don't want paved trails, a degradation of the land.

The bicycle industry now sells nontoxic chain lube, non-toxic, citrus-based degreaser, and lights built to use rechargeable batteries. Ask for these items at the bike shop you frequent. Finally, eat organically and low on the food chain—the world is overcrowded, not just your favorite primitive trail.

The rules

- Don't leave any trace: no Power Bar wrappers, no treadmarks on delicate trails, no toilet paper, no cigarette butts, and no clear plastic strips from the back of inner-tube patches.
- Don't skid—ever. Don't ride on poorly made trails, on wet trails, or when the earth is liable to be marred by tires. Walk around all delicate areas.
- Respect all other trail users. Yield the right of way to everyone, including hikers, runners, other bicyclists, motorcycles, and horses.
- Stop and dismount when you encounter horses. Stand on the downhill side of the trail, and talk to the horse and rider as they pass.
- Ride in control. For your safety and others, master low-speed riding.
- Respect wildlife (you are in their home!) and livestock.
- Never come screaming around blind corners at 50 miles per hour screaming "Mountain biker from hell!"

WHOSE LAND IS THIS ANYWAY?

Most of the rides in *Kissing the Trail* are confined to public land. But some rides travel over informal community trails on privately owned land. The trails in this book that do cross private land have a long history of community use. Some land owners have posted signs that allow nonintrusive, daytime use by bicyclists and other users; other owners allow cyclists to use the land but haven't gone to the trouble of putting up signs. Owners can be fickle—allowing use one day, tacking up no-trespassing signs the next. If the property is not signed, or you are not sure of its status, you should obtain permission from the owner before riding. Obviously, when faced with no-trespassing signs—especially the tin version pounded by bullets—it's prudent to find another ride. The author does not condone or encourage trespassing onto private property. *Kissing the Trail* simply points out areas where bicyclists, equestrians, and pedestrians already spend time, usually because these areas are beautiful, primitive, and close to urban areas.

Despite the beauty, it's time to turn around.

As of January 1993, none of the trails in this book cross through any front yards. However, most of the private land mentioned in this book will be developed within the next fifteen years, some of it over the next two years. Given this, a ride that doesn't cross any front yards in January 1993 might do so in October 1993. The incentive here is huge: enjoy these areas now, for they will soon be cement. If a particular ride has been encroached upon by development—and it can happen quickly—select a different ride.

Trails that have been used over the years for nonimpacting recreation by the community should be preserved, whether the property is public or private. If trails exist in an area scheduled to be developed, the public should demand that developers preserve those trails when the digging begins. When public jurisdictions acquire land, issue use permits, or implement regional plans, trails should be kept intact. Trail systems should be expanded whenever possible—we all own our public lands, and we all have a vested interest in the use of private land, especially private land with a history of community use. If you have a problem with the way some land you cherish is being used or abused, write or call your elected representative or the land manager for the area in question (see page 33).

MAN'S BEST FRIEND: DUCT TAPE

It's 6 p.m., and you're ten miles out in the backcountry. You have paid your dues for five hours, and now it's time for the downhill plunge (controlled, of course); you figure you can still make it for your 8 p.m. dinner date. Unfortunately, your derailleur hit a rock a half-mile back and bent a little. You didn't notice. But when you shift down to climb a short hill, your derailleur shifts past the biggest cog—cunkkk—into the spokes of your rear wheel. The bike stops instantly, catapulting you toward that shrubbery on the side of the trail. Whoa, whoa, whoa. No physical damage (that's for the "Safety" chapter to handle), but your derailleur looks like a worrier's paper clip, and several of the spokes on your rear wheel look like two-hour linguini. Major malfunction. If you don't have a tool kit and some extra spokes, you'll probably spend the night in the woods and, worse yet, miss that dinner reservation. But if you have the right tools and know how to use them, you can probably still make it back for that fettucine primavera.

When you bicycle into the backcountry, damage to either you or your bike can mean a long walk, especially with a bike on your shoulder. Always carry a tool kit so you can fix anything from nine flat tires to a broken chain. Sometimes you need some imagination to concoct short-term fixes for uncommon problems. The key is to use your imagination. One time, a friend filled his tire with pine cones to finish the ride because he didn't have any spare inner tubes. When I rode around the United States a number of years ago, I found that almost anything could be doctored, one way or another, if I had the four essentials—duct tape, vice grips, Super Glue, bailing wire (these four items also kept my '69 Dodge Coronet running for years).

Of course some problems are even too big for duct tape, vice grips, Super Glue, and bailing wire. You may find yourself ten miles out in the woods with a broken frame, a pretzeled wheel, or some other catastrophic failure. Unfortunately, there's not a pannier bag big enough to carry enough duct tape to fix these types of problems—thus the advice to take along water, food, flashlight, lighter, and extra clothes. Here is a suggested list of tools. But remember: Everyone's bike is different, so you should customize this list so it makes sense for your bike.

Recommended tools

- pump
- patch kit
- extra tube
- tire irons
- extra spokes
- freewheel remover
- spoke wrench
- chain tool
- Allen wrenches
- needle-nose pliers
- crescent wrench
- screwdriver
- spare brake cable
- rag

Photo by M. Angela Castañeda

A quick repair on a dusty descent

LOST WITH ELVIS

Every summer people get eaten by bears gone berserk, miners spot Elvis on horseback, Bigfoot performs a brief cameo, and then the tabloids read "Astronauts Discover Mountain Bike in Orbit." It's a sad summertime fact: Many people end up on the wrong trail, headed in the wrong direction just as the sun begins to set.

Getting lost in the woods while riding a bike is easier than you might think, and much easier than while hiking. When you hike, you move slowly and methodically, watching for small bends in the trail, cairns, and other trail markers. While mountain biking, you can ride by an unnoticed cairn or turn in the trail because you were negotiating your way down a technical section of trail. So stop and pay attention to your surroundings, watch the lay of the land,

Making notes on a new trail, circa 1898

stop and review the maps. This is not Magic Mountain, and no steel rails will return you safely to the beginning of the ride.

To avoid getting lost: **1.** Gain an adequate knowledge of the area before leaving home. **2.** Take a map, compass, and the skills to use them. **3.** Pay attention while riding along the trail. **4.** Stay home if severe weather is forecast. **5.** Use good sense and stay on the main trail: faint trails, animal paths, abandoned railroad grades, and logging roads are everywhere. In some areas, especially near mines, timber harvests, or in off-road vehicle areas, old jeep trails are as common as pine needles. Your brain must sift through all the information—maps and trail descriptions, the sun, your compass, the lay of the land—and you must decide *not to get lost*.

If you do find yourself lost, don't panic. If you panic, you might as well subtract a few thousand dollars from your checkbook ledger for all the helicopter fuel it will take to find you. (Sorry, no IRA this year.) If lost, put on all your warm clothes; try to relax and think with your cortex rather than your thalamus.

RIDING TECHNIQUES

Many of the rides in *Kissing the Trail* don't require extreme riding skill or Herculean fitness; others do. The technical advice that follows is for the rider who wants to smoothly matriculate from road riding to trail riding. Unfortunately, riding skills develop by trial and error. These suggestions ought to shorten the learning curve and minimize the number of times you eat dirt.

CADENCE: As a rule, it's best to pedal 70 to 100 rotations per minute while riding a bike. This can seem awkwardly fast if you're not used to "spinning" so quickly. But a healthy cadence is the easiest way to keep your legs fresh for the longest time possible. Slow, laborious pedal strokes strain muscles, tiring them for the miles ahead. In the mountains the cadence rule doesn't always apply: some climbs are too steep, some downhills are too scary, and the really tricky spots are too tricky. Using toe clips helps keep up a good, even, circular cadence (in addition to keeping your feet on the pedals). Also, a good cadence is easiest when your seat has been adjusted properly. Put the seat up high enough so your legs become nearly straight at the bottom of the pedal stroke: a 5 percent bend at the knee is about right. If the trail isn't steep or tricky, try for a cadence of 70 to 100 rotations per minute.

DOWNHILL: The idea on any downhill pitch is not to flip forward over the front wheel. To accomplish this, adjust your seat down an inch or two and sit back to lower your center of gravity. In extreme cases, move your butt so it is actually behind the seat. Keep your arms and legs slightly bent, not locked—your arms and legs act as shock absorbers. Keep your hands firmly and consistently on the brakes; you'll get nowhere waving one arm around like a cowboy. Don't brake suddenly, especially with the front brake. Here's the Catch-22 of braking: The front brake does most of the real braking, *but* you have more precise steering *and* you're less likely to flip if there is less pressure applied to the front brake. Remember speed is the most hazardous bicycling condition—it's difficult to get hurt at 1 mile per hour; at 20 miles per hour it's all too easy.

UPHILL: The idea here is to get to the top the easiest way possible. During the transition between level or downhill riding and uphill, shift to a lower gear *before* you lose momentum. By maintaining a quick, even cadence throughout the transition, the hill will seem smooth and your legs won't lock as readily. During a steep

Finishing a log crossing. Don't try this helmet-less trick at home.

climb, stay seated so your weight stays over the rear wheel to keep it from spinning. At the same time, however, make sure enough of your weight remains forward so the front wheel doesn't pop up unexpectedly. If you don't make it to the top of a hill, it usually won't be because the wild pigs got you; rather, it will be because your rear wheel spun out and you tipped over. On longer, more gradual hills, stand up occasionally—for power and muscle variety—but be careful not to lose traction on the rear wheel. And never let your rear wheel damage the earth—always try to avoid skidding on the descents or spinning the rear wheel on power ascents. Finally, concentrate on deep, relaxed breathing; avoid locomotive breathing.

WATER: Inevitably, the mountain biker will come forehead to forehead with a body of water that needs to be navigated. And sometimes "navigate" is the right word when water reaches the seat post, and you're thrashing and churning to stay vertical, hoping the current doesn't sweep the bike away. When you encounter a stream, keep these things in mind: **1.** It's smart to know what the bottom of the stream looks like; aim for the smoothest route across. **2.** Don't let the shock of entering the water freeze your legs; keep pedaling until you reach the opposite side. **3.** Pay attention to the environment; don't rage across small, delicate, dirt-bedded creeks—stop and carry your bike across. This is critical during the fall when salmon are spawning, since even very shallow creeks can be salmon habitat.

TECHNICAL RIDING: Rocks, roots, tight corners, switchbacks, billiard balls of horse pucky, drop-offs, encroaching foliage, gravel, logs, other trail users, salamanders, all shapes and sizes of puddles—needless to say, there are times and places when the riding becomes technical and exemplary riding skills help tremendously. Although the proper ratio of balance and riding experience usually determines whether you'll get through a difficult section, sometimes a little reminder helps. **1.** Try standing up on the pedals at times. **2.** When it's rough, keep an iron grip on the handlebars. **3.** Grip the seat with your thighs on downhills. **4.** Always use your arms and legs as shock absorbers, not rebar. **5.** Keep pedaling! The best way to ride over or around obstacles is to do it.

WALKING YOUR BIKE: Walk the bike? This sounds like a non sequitur, like combining the words "mountain" and "bike" sounded, say, fifteen years ago. The whole point of "bicycle" is that walking becomes extinct. Not. If you want to ride a mountain bike in the woods, you're bound to do some walking. Absolutely every serious mountain biker walks at some time, usually after trying to ride over a bus-sized rock or around a pit of poisonous snakes. Even the racers walk. Walking up a hill will almost always help extend the energy and spring in your already knotted legs, and it will make the remainder of the ride more enjoyable. Also, be cool to the earth: Walk to avoid damaging the trail.

BUYING A BICYCLE

The first decision you will need to make concerns the size of the check you want to write. Mountain bikes range in price from just under $200 to well over $4,000. How much to spend depends on your checkbook balance *and* the type of riding that you plan to do. Since we're talking about mountain bikes, I assume that you'll want to take the beast out onto some dirt roads and trails. For a basic mountain bike that performs with some degree of precision on dirt roads and trails, you'll need to wring at least $350 from your wallet. At this price you can expect a lightweight frame, alloy wheels, and an adequate set of components. In addition to the bike and the sales tax, you probably want a lock, a helmet, a pump, and some other goodies which can easily surpass $150.

As the price goes up, two things happen—first, the weight of the bike drops and, second, the components last longer, perform better, and look like they came from Saks rather than K Mart. After the mountain bike passes the $1,200 threshold, you are paying for art. Up until that point, though, mountain bikes really do get lighter and better, and the average rider can feel the difference. Counterpoint: A $300 bike will get you there. In fact, I researched two mountain bike guides on bicycles that cost less than $400.

COMPONENTS: Components consist of everything but the frame and the wheels. A bike that costs more will come fitted with better components. Two things: **1.** Ask the salesperson to describe the differences between components on separate bikes. Then go to another store and ask someone else the same question. Does it really matter that the chain on one bike is better than the chain on another? Look closely at the components—do they appear sturdy or cheap? If you are unsure why a part is attached to the bicycle you want to buy, have the salesperson explain its function. The more time you spend checking out a bicycle before you buy it, the less lingering anger you'll have over the next few years. **2.** Give the brakes and derailleurs a good workout on the test ride.

THE FRAME AND WHEELS: A lightweight frame and set of alloy wheels combine to make a more responsive, less fatiguing ride. The lighter the bicycle, the easier it is to ride. The difference is dramatic when maneuvering around obstacles on the trail, climbing hills, and accelerating. Most frames are made of either chrome-molybdenum steel, aluminum, or a combination of the two. The ride, or feel, of the frame depends on the materials, the architecture of the frame (tube lengths and angles), and your body. Although all frames look similar, just an inch here or there can feel much better or worse, especially if you have an extra long pair of legs, a short torso, or if one arm is longer than the other. Some frames provide a soft, comfortable ride; others offer a stiff, manic ride. Which feels best to you? Test ride, test ride, test ride.

SIZING A BIKE: Sizing a mountain bike is more complex than sizing a road bicycle. When you stand over a road bike, you should be able to lift it up about an inch; with a mountain bike, the distance should be three or four inches, depending on your riding style. Choose a slightly larger bike if you plan to do most of your riding on the road, a smaller one if you want to concentrate on off-road riding. Smaller frames are lighter, stronger, and flex less than larger frames. Sometimes, however, a bigger frame just feels more comfortable. To add to the confusion, mountain bikes are measured in various ways, so a 20-inch bike might be labeled a 19-inch bike by one company, but a 21-inch by another. Be sure the salesperson fits you to each bike before the test ride and adjusts the seat properly. The real test is, of course, the test ride.

THE TEST RIDE: Once you have decided on a price and the size, and you have selected several bicycles that seem right, then buy the one that looks the coolest. Hello, have you been listening? It's time for the test ride. Take this part seriously; don't stop by the store after work, planning to ride the bike in your suit. Wear cycling clothes, and take your time.

When you ride the bike out of the store, don't just ride it around the block; try to ride the bike as though you already own it. Ride up and down steep hills, and see if the bike responds the way you like to ride. Ask yourself some questions during the short time you have with the bike. Does your torso feel too scrunched or too stretched out from the seat to the handlebars? How does it turn and shift and brake and accelerate? Some bikes will feel methodical but stable, other bikes will feel nimble but skittish. It's difficult to extrapolate from a short test ride to an eight-hour journey, but intuition is a pretty good judge. Buy what feels best.

Test riding a new bike

TRAINING

Everyone wants to be able to hop on the bike and ride for miles without fatigue. This is impossible. For many, a day of mountain biking means an evening of zoning out in front of the television. But it is possible to get into good enough shape so that you can go dancing after dinner rather than groping for the nearest couch. There are two key elements to mountain biking with less fatigue. Riding skill is the first element. If you are a beginning rider, you expend lots of energy worrying, gripping the handle bars too tightly, maneuvering around small obstacles, and starting and stopping. The only advice I can give is to rewind to the riding techniques section where it says improving is all about trial and error.

Being in shape is the second element. But being in shape doesn't mean riding a zillion miles at top speed; it means molding your fitness so that you work on strength and endurance—and you need both out on the trail. If the endurance part is missing, you'll bonk after an hour or two and your friends will abandon you because of your grumpiness; if the strength part is missing, your leg muscles will tear to shreds on the first hard climb, and your friends will leave you because you are riding so slowly. Start out with road rides or trail rides known to be easy, so you don't overdo it the first few times out. To improve endurance, ride on the flats for many hours with your pulse at or above 130 beats per minute. Although you should keep a quick cadence on these rides, you ought to be able to hold a conversation most of the way. To gain strength, go on rides that emphasize sprints, hills, and some larger gears. These rides should be varied; at times your pulse should reach 90 percent of your maximum (220 minus your age). At the top of each hill you should be gasping for breath, unable to utter a word. But be sure to rest enough at the top so that you have use of every faculty on the descent. I recommend putting in at least a month of quality endurance riding before you begin the strength rides. To stay in mountain-biking shape, you need to exercise at least four times each week, three of which should be bicycling.

VICES: Now that you are in shape, I'll try to wreck it by offering donuts and ropes of licorice. Junk food is the pirate of the food world, plundering our bodies with blank calories, heaps of sodium, and buckets of fat. Athletes like to argue that exercise mediates the downside of these rogue foods. Olympic marathon runner Don Kardong has said that without ice cream there would be darkness and chaos in the world. My question is: What about hamburgers, chips, donuts, red wine, and bulk cookies?

Indeed, no rules regarding vices and mountain biking exist, although many a dogmatic bicyclist will lecture you differently. Plato urged us to search for a golden mean, a point between excesses, between many vices and none.

MUD MAINTENANCE

How do you keep the steed running smoothly? Although all bikes will inevitably go out of tune from rust, cracked rubber, lack of lubrication, and stretched cables, there's only one, big problem about keeping your mountain bicycle running: mud. Mud—water and dirt—causes brakes to fail, derailleurs to stop functioning, bearings to grind to square cubes, and it weighs the bike down. (Some cyclecross racers swap bikes every couple of miles during a race because of the extra two pounds of mud that the bike collects.) Riders run the gamut from those who have anxiety attacks when the first mud strikes their cycle to those who never clean their bikes at all. One of the debates centers on the use of a hose to clean the bike. Some shops tell you to let the mud dry, then wipe it down with a heavy brush, so you won't taint your bike with water. Much too complicated and time consuming. Besides, since my bike gets drenched during rides

Getting dirty near Novelty Hill

and soaked while on top of my car, it doesn't seem like a little hose action will hurt. Go ahead, hose the thing down until the dirt is gone, then dry it off with a rag. Just try not to aim the water into the hubs. When the bearings grind square, replace them.

As far as other bicycle maintenance goes, usually the bike will let you know when things aren't running smoothly. Headsets, bottom brackets, cables, brake pads, tires, the chain, the square bearings, the wheels, and the freewheel are components to watch. When it looks or feels as though something's not working so well, figure out what's wrong and fix it. Either fix it yourself or take it to a qualified mechanic. Remember: Every bike can and should run smoothly. It's a lot less painful to extract a twenty from your wallet now than to stand on the trail in the rain, looking at a nonfunctioning bike.

What about clothes? Questions about laundry prove I have digressed a long way; however, there is not enough bleach on the planet to keep your riding socks white.

Maintenance suggestions
- Always keep your chain clean and lubricated.
- Always keep the brake pad surface flat (file them down) and brakes adjusted.
- Always keep the wheels true.
- Replace your chain every 800 miles.
- Replace your freewheel when the teeth look like V-necks rather than crew necks.
- Replace tires, cables, and wheels when they look and/or feel worn.
- Repack bearings in hubs, bottom bracket, and headset twice a year.
- Replace socks daily.

MOUNTAIN BICYCLE ADVOCACY

Hearing from constituents makes a difference. Legislation is passed or discarded largely due to the number of calls and letters lawmakers receive on a given issue. Even non-elected officials make major decisions based on public input. The squeaky wheel does get the attention. If you have a question, a problem, or any kind of comment, call.

Emergencies   911

Weather Service   (206) 526-6087

Publications
Northwest Cyclist Magazine   (206) 286-8566
The Bicycle Paper   (206) 523-3470

Clubs
Backcountry Bicycle Trails Club   (206) 283-2995
Cascade Bicycle Club   (206) 522-3222
International Mountain Bike Association   (818) 792-8830

Jurisdictions
Seattle City Parks   (206) 684-4075
Seattle Open Space   (206) 684-0777
King County Parks   (206) 296-4232
King County Open Space   (206) 296-7800
City of Issaquah Parks   (206) 391-1008
City of Redmond Parks   (206) 556-2313
Washington State Dept. of Natural Resources (800) 527-3305
National Parks   (206) 220-7450
National Forest Service   (206) 220-7450
   North Bend Ranger District   (206) 888-1421
   White River Ranger District   (206) 825-6585
   Wenatchee Ranger District   (509) 662-4335

Political Offices
United States Senate   (202) 224-3121
United States House of Representatives   (202) 225-3121
Washington State Switchboard   (800) 321-2808
WA State Legislative Hotline (in session) (800) 562-6000
King County Council   (206) 296-1000
Seattle City Council   (206) 684-8888
White House Switchboard (ask for Al Gore) (202) 456-1414

Ride 1 ✿ ✿ ✿ ✿

THE LAST DIRT TRAIL

Checklist: 29.5 miles, One Way; dirt trails, dirt roads, paved roads
Duration: 5–8 hours
Hill factor: rolling hills, some steep sections, some walking
Skill level: advanced
Season: all year
Maps: USGS Bellevue North, USGS Bellevue South
Ownership: public, private
User density: low to high depending on section; equestrians, bicyclists, hikers
Hazards: mud, getting lost, fatigue, becoming a mountain-bike evangelist

Prelude

The Last Dirt Trail epitomizes the best and worst in the current state of mountain bicycling in Western Washington. The best: to discover that there is a series of primarily dirt trails through lush forests from Woodinville's Sammamish River Trail to Issaquah's Alps. If that weren't enough, the Last Dirt Trail is also known as the String of Pearls because it connects six great mountain bicycling areas—the Redmond Watershed, Novelty Hill, the Northwest Passage, Beaver Lake East, Grand Ridge, and Tiger Mountain. It could be the only trail you'd ever need. The worst: the Last Dirt Trail highlights the intense land-use struggle for undeveloped land on the east side of Lake Washington and on the Sammamish Plateau. Although it might be the only trail you need now, it may disappear in the near future. Significant sections of this 30-mile ride pass through the 7,000 acres of private land scheduled for real estate development. Most of this development will occur over the next fifteen years. The second assault on trails comes from other user groups determined to ban bicycles from public land. Much of Tiger Mountain and the rest of the Issaquah Alps are off limits to mountain bicyclists, and the exclusions could expand. As you ride through this beautiful, forested land, ask yourself how you can help protect open space in Western Washington.

To get there

Take Interstate 405 to Exit 20B. Travel east on N.E. 124th Street to Highway 202 (the Redmond-Woodinville Road). Turn left on 202. Then take another left upon reaching N.E. 145th Street. Before crossing the Sammamish River, find a gravel parking lot on the right. Remember, this is a One Way ride, so if you plan to do the entire ride, you should park a second car in Issaquah.

The ride

Begin from the gravel parking area south of Woodinville, on the corner of N.E. 145th Street and 148th Ave. N.E., across the Sammamish River from the Chateau Ste. Michelle winery. The Sammamish Trail borders the parking lot. Begin the ride traveling north on the trail. Ride to the Tolt Pipeline Trail, **.3 mile**. Turn right onto the gravely Tolt Pipeline Trail. At **.65 mile**, cross the Redmond-Woodinville Road, then begin a very steep climb that may require walking. The hill ends at **1 mile**. At **1.15 miles**, the trail seems to end at a bluff. Find a steep, single-track trail on the right that drops down to a road. Be careful because the trail drops right to the edge of the road and cars come around the corner quickly. It's prudent to walk this short section of trail. Look to the left and find the pipeline trail continuing east, about 20 yards up the road. Immediately, the trail climbs again: this may be another push. At **2.1 miles**, reach the top of the second hill. At **4.5 miles**, after numerous gates

Near Novelty Hill on the Last Dirt Trail

Photo by Greg Strong

and road crossings, begin climbing again. Don't ride through any of the streams along the Tolt Pipeline Trail because salmon spawn in some of these streams and salmon have a hard enough time these days without mountain bikers raging through their natural incubators. **Whoa!** At **6.5 miles**, find a slight trail on the right side of the Tolt Pipeline Trail. This is easy to miss. Turn right and ride down the sometimes muddy and overgrown single track.

At **6.7 miles**, the trail ends at a wider trail: take a left. Ride this old railroad grade to an intersection at the **7.5-mile** mark. Turn left, pedaling up the hill. (Pearl #1, the Redmond Watershed, page 69, can be accessed by continuing straight at this intersection.) At **7.7 miles** the trail forks: take the left fork. From here, stay on the main jeep road, passing several lesser roads on the left and right. At **8.9 miles**, reach Novelty Hill Road. From here, cross the road, turn right, ride about 20 yards, then turn left onto a trail that cuts away from the road. At **9.1 miles**, the muddy, dark trail meets a set of power lines: turn left, riding down the dirt road under the power lines. (Pearl #2, the Novelty Hill ride, page 75, begins close by.) When the road divides, **9.5 miles**, take a sharp right into the woods, away from the power lines. Ride past a rusted van and a trail on the left. Stay on the main trail here. At **9.6 miles**, pass a trail on the left. At **10.3 miles**, turn left at a four-way intersection. At **11.2 miles**, reach a T: turn left. At **11.4 miles**, turn right at the fork. At **12.1 miles**, turn left at another T.

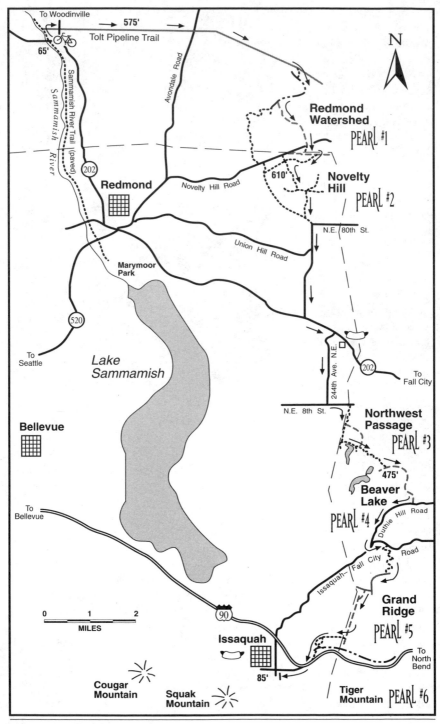

To Woodinville

575'

Tolt Pipeline Trail

65'

Sammamish River Trail (paved)

Sammamish River

Avondale Road

N

Redmond Watershed

PEARL #1

202

Redmond

Novelty Hill Road

610'

Novelty Hill

PEARL #2

N.E. 80th St.

Union Hill Road

Marymoor Park

520

To Seattle

Lake Sammamish

Bellevue

To Fall City

202

244th Ave. N.E.

N.E. 8th St.

Northwest Passage

PEARL #3

475'

Beaver Lake

PEARL #4

Duthie Hill Road

To Bellevue

Issaquah–Fall City Road

Grand Ridge

PEARL #5

0   1   2
MILES

90

Issaquah

85'

To North Bend

Cougar Mountain

Squak Mountain

Tiger Mountain   PEARL #6

At **12.3 miles**, reach N.E. 80th Street and 238th Ave. N.E. Turn right and ride down 238th. At the **12.9-mile** mark, the pavement forks—stay on 238th, the left fork. Stay on 238th, which becomes 236th, until it ends at Highway 202, the Redmond–Fall City Road. Turn left onto 202. Upon reaching 244th Ave. N.E., turn right, **15.4 miles**. Quickly, the road begins ascending a steep hill. (If you stay on 202 another 200 yards, you'll find a store with terrible water and excellent Jo-Jo's.) After the first climb up 244th the road rolls along to an intersection at **17.2 miles**. Turn left onto N.E. 8th Street. Ride down the hill until you get to a set of power lines that run perpendicular to the road, **17.7 miles**. At the power lines, find a trail on the right that follows the power lines. (Pearl #3, the Northwest Passage, page 77, begins here.)

From N.E. 8th Street and the power lines, pedal up the trail, which varies from single track to jeep trail to gravel road. At **17.8 miles**, the trail veers into the woods on the left. At **18.3 miles**, a dirt road cuts back to the left; continue on the main road along the power lines. Several pedal strokes farther, the road divides again; take the easier, main road to the right (the two roads converge again after less than a quarter-mile). Over the next one-quarter mile, several trails and an old road exit to the right and make for interesting exploration. Instead stay on the main road. At **18.6 miles**, five feet after the fifth power-line tower, take the lesser, grassy road on the left, passing under the wires. The trail narrows as it ducks into the woods. At **18.8 miles**, the trail divides: continue straight—the left fork—over roots, through mud pockets and underbrush, and around fallen trees. After **19.3 miles**, the trail widens slightly, then forks again. (The left fork will return you to the power lines in .8 mile, a half-mile from N.E. 8th Street.) Take the right fork and ride quietly into a wonderful old cedar grove, scheduled to be the 17th hole of the Beaver Lake Estates golf course. From here, stay on the main trail as it snakes through the forest.

Negotiating an October puddle. Don't be a nudnick; wear a helmet.

At the **20.7-mile** mark the single track ends at a primitive jeep trail. Turn right, riding up a gentle grade. (Pearl #4, Beaver Lake East, page 87, travels this trail.) At **20.9 miles**, pass a dirt road that exits right—stay left. Continue on the jeep trail as it traverses downhill to another jeep trail at **21.1 miles**. To the right you'll see a fence and a paved street. Turn left and ride up the jeep trail. At **21.2 miles**, pass a road on the left. Just beyond this point, pass a single track on the right, continue straight along the main jeep trail. At **21.4 miles**, pass another single track on the right. Several pedal strokes further, pass another jeep trail on the left. Stay on the main trail. At **22.2 miles**, pass another jeep trail left, then drop down a short hill to a fence and a pasture beyond the fence, **22.3 miles**. From here, turn right and follow the trail to the Duthie Hill Road, 50 yards away.

Turning right on the road, you'll probably be thankful for the smooth pavement after 22 miles of riding. Ride along the Duthie Hill Road until it intersects with the Issaquah–Fall City Road, **23.8 miles**. Turn left on this road, pedal about a hundred yards, and find a faint trail that exits from the road on the right. Turn in here, into the seeming brush. **Whoa**, this is a difficult trail to find and it's technical as well. At **24.3 miles**, the single track meets a dirt road. Turn left; the way soon becomes a jeep trail and drops steadily down a hill. At **24.5 miles**, just as the descent levels and the trail bears to the left, the trail becomes a single track. Be sure to stay on the main trail. After a short stretch of single track, cross a creek, and follow the trail up a hill to the left. The hill is short, but the trail remains tricky, through dark forest, dropping and climbing, until it pops out onto a jeep trail at **25 miles**. Turn right down the primitive dirt road.

The road becomes wider and more traveled. When the road stops at a T, **25.25 miles**, turn left, uphill. Just up the hill, reach an intersection and turn right. At **25.6 miles**, after dropping quickly down the gravel road, turn uphill to the left to a green gate. Several pedal strokes farther, emerge from the woods under a set of power lines, **25.7 miles**, and turn left. (Pearl #5, Grand Ridge, page 82, can be accessed from these power lines.) Ride along the power lines to the **27-mile** mark, just before the power lines drop over the edge of the bluff (pass one trail on the right and several on the left before reaching this point). Turn right on the trail just before the edge. When the trail crosses under a second set of power lines at **27.3 miles**, continue straight up the hill through the intersection and back into the woods. At **27.5 miles**, turn left; at **27.9 miles**, after a descent, turn left again. From here, follow the trail as it drops steeply down to the railroad grade at **28.25 miles**. (Pearl #6, Tiger Mountain, page 101, utilizes this trail.) Turn right, down the railroad grade; at **28.5 miles** take the left fork away from the railroad grade, down toward Interstate 90. At **28.7 miles**, find a rickety footbridge that leads to an area under the highway. Scramble under the highway and reach Sunset Way at **28.75 miles**. Turn right and ride down into Issaquah. Reach Front Street at **29.4 miles** and arrive at the old Issaquah railroad station parking lot at **29.5 miles**.

Ride 2 ✿✿✿

MIDDLE FORK OF THE SNOQUALMIE RIVER

Checklist: 6 miles, Out & Back; dirt trails
Duration: 2–4 hours
Hill factor: rolling with a number of short, steep sections
Skill level: advanced
Season: summer, early fall
Maps: Green Trails Skykomish, Green Trails Mount Si
Ownership: U.S. Forest Service
User density: medium; hikers, bicyclists
Hazards: slippery bridges, sensitive trail

Prelude

The Middle Fork of the Snoqualmie River is rugged and beautiful. Cascading creeks and huge ancient trees lace the edges of the powerful river. This is a delicate trail so please use caution; walking is necessary in a number of sections to prevent trail damage.

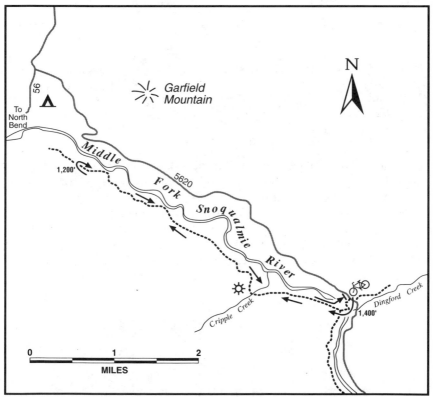

To get there

Take Interstate 90 to the Edgewick Exit, #34, and turn north. Drive .4 mile, and take a right onto S.E. Middle Fork Road. One mile farther, 1.4 miles from I-90, take the right fork. At 2.7 miles, the road becomes dirt. From here stay on the main road. When the road forks again at 10.3 miles, stay right alongside the river. At 12.4 miles, stay left on the main road, #56. At 13 miles take the right fork, winding up the hill. Park at the Dingford Creek Trailhead, 18 miles from I-90. Warning: This rough and formidable road has a tendency to wash out.

The ride

Middle Fork of the Snoqualmie River on a fall morning

On the river side of the road, across from the Dingford Creek Trailhead, find the Middle Fork Trail, #1003, on the right. Take this trail which quickly drops down toward the river. At **.2 mile** reach a suspension bridge. After crossing the bridge the trail divides. Turn right and ride up the hill. Some walking is necessary. Be very careful of this trail: it's a pine-needle trail and susceptible to damage. From here, ride down river through heavy forest on the narrow, dirt trail, crossing several bridges. Renovation is being done on this trail. As of autumn 1992, the trail was only maintained about **3 miles** from the suspension bridge. Ride to the end of the maintained trail, turn around, and retrace your steps for a total of **6 miles**.

Ride 3 ✹ ✹✹✹ ✹

GOLDMYER HOTSPRINGS I

Checklist: 10.6 miles, Loop; dirt trails, dirt roads
Duration: 2–5 hours
Hill factor: consistent climb to Goldmyer, many steep sections with walks
Skill level: expert
Season: summer, early fall
Maps: Green Trails Skykomish, Green Trails Snoqualmie Pass
Ownership: public, private
User density: medium to low; hikers, bicyclists, cars
Hazards: cross 3 creeks, ford 2 rivers, climb over avalanche; cars on road

Prelude

This is one of the most beautiful areas described in *Kissing the Trail*. The route parallels the majestic Middle Fork, skirting pockets of old growth, up a wild, unmaintained trail. This is a delicate trail so please use caution; walking is necessary through many sections to prevent trail damage. Since Goldmyer is operated by a private, non-profit group, reservations and some cash are required if you want to soak in the hot pools. Warning: The ride may be longer than posted here because the rough and formidable road has a tendency to wash out. For road conditions and Goldmyer information, call (206) 789-5631.

To get there

Take Interstate 90 to the Edgewick Exit, #34, and turn north. Drive .4 mile, and take a right onto S.E. Middle Fork Road. One mile farther, 1.4 miles from I-90, take the right fork. At 2.7 miles, the road becomes dirt. From here stay on the main road. When the road forks again at 10.3 miles, stay right alongside the river. At 12.4 miles, stay left on the main road, #56. At 13 miles take the right fork, winding up the hill. Park at the Dingford Creek Trailhead, 18 miles from I-90.

The ride

On the river side of the road, across from the Dingford Creek Trailhead, find the Middle Fork Trail, #1003, on the right. Take this trail which quickly drops down toward the river. At **.2 mile** reach a suspension bridge, cross bridge and come to T. Turn left and ride up the hill. Some walking. Be very careful of this trail: it's a pine-needle trail and susceptible to damage. To prevent damage, you should walk many sections of trail even though they seem ridable. Check out the enormous cedar trees—genuine old growth before your eyes. Unfortunately, most of the forest was chopped early in the century so the big trees are few and far between. At **.3 mile** get to the top and come to an intersection—go left toward Snow Lake, upstream. At **1.7 miles** reach a stream; careful, there is no bridge. The trail becomes very steep.

After the climb, at **1.9 miles**, the trail levels upon reaching an old logging railroad grade. At **3 miles**, take the left fork, continuing up the Middle Fork Trail, #1003. At **3.4 miles**, you have to climb over an enormous log jam: tedious and dangerous. Cross rugged streams at **3.9 and 4.5 miles**. At a deteriorating sign at the edge of Burnt Boot Creek, the trail is washed out and seems to disappear altogether. Cross Burnt Boot Creek here and find the trail on the opposite bank, **5.2 miles**. Finding the trail across the creek can be a stretch. Once you find the trail, turn right, and immediately you'll see the caretaker's cabin for Goldmyer Hot Springs, **5.5 miles**. Stop here and enquire within if you want to soak in the hotsprings.

From the cabin, take the trail past the bell—left—and ride about one-quarter-mile, staying on the main trail, to the Middle Fork of the Snoqualmie River. Wade through the river, and find the road on the other side, **5.8 miles**. Take the primitive road on the right. It bends around to the left and then meets the main road at **6 miles**. From here turn left, downstream. At **10.5 miles**, cross the Dingford Creek bridge, lovely spot. At **10.6 miles**, reach the Middle Fork Trailhead and the car.

Cyclist awed by a massvie cedar

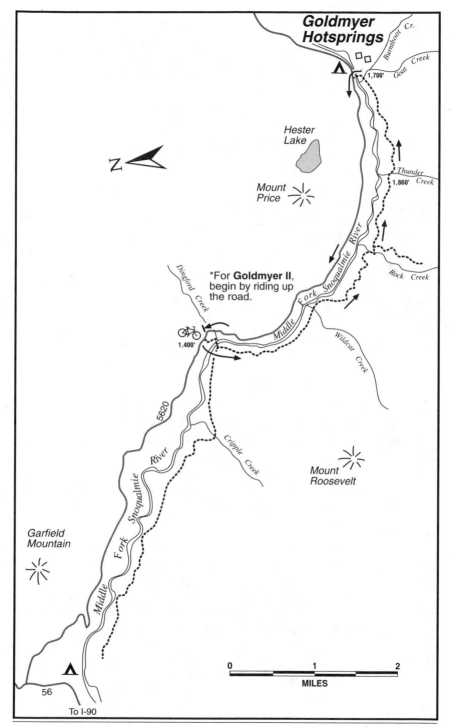

Goldmyer
Hotsprings

Burntboot Cr.

Goat Creek

1,700'

Hester
Lake

Thunder Creek

1,860'

Mount
Price

Rock Creek

Middle Fork Snoqualmie River

Dingford Creek

*For **Goldmyer II**,
begin by riding up
the road.

1,400'

Wildcat Creek

5620

Middle Fork Snoqualmie River

Cripple Creek

Mount
Roosevelt

Garfield
Mountain

Middle Fork Snoqualmie River

N

0   1   2
MILES

56

To I-90

Ride 4 ✹✹

GOLDMYER HOTSPRINGS II

Checklist: 10 miles, Out & Back; dirt trails, dirt roads
Duration: 1–2 hours
Hill factor: consistent climb to Goldmyer
Skill level: beginner, with some rough sections of road
Season: summer, early fall
Maps: Green Trails Skykomish, Green Trails Snoqualmie Pass
Ownership: U.S. Forest Service, private
User density: medium; bicyclists, cars
Hazards: cars on road

Prelude

This version is an easier and shorter way up to the hotsprings. The sacrifice is that it is a dirt road the entire way, so you may be dueling with automobiles. Since Goldmyer is operated by a private, nonprofit group, reservations and some cash are required if you want to soak in the hot pools. Warning: The ride may be longer than posted here because the rough and formidable road has a tendency to wash out. For road conditions and Goldmyer information, call (206) 789-5631. It's a lovely ride, even if a hot soak isn't part of the plan.

To get there

Take Interstate 90 to the Edgewick Exit, #34, and turn north. Drive .4 mile, and take a right onto S.E. Middle Fork Road. One mile farther, 1.4 miles from I-90, take the right fork. At 2.7 miles, the road becomes dirt. From here stay on the main road. When the road forks again at 10.3 miles, stay right alongside the river. At 12.4 miles, stay left on the main road, #56. At 13 miles take the right fork, winding up the hill. Park at the Dingford Creek Trailhead, 18 miles from I-90.

The ride

From the Dingford Creek Trailhead, ride up the road that parallels the Middle Fork of the Snoqualmie River. The road climbs gradually with some hearty grades. At **4.8 miles**, the road forks. Take the lesser road to the right, which winds down to the river. Ford the river, and find the trail on the opposite bank. Follow the main trail for one-quarter mile, bypassing campsite spurs, to the Goldmyer Hotsprings cabin, **5 miles**. When you're done soaking, retrace your steps for a total of **10 miles**.

The map

For the map to this ride see the previous page.

Ride 5 🌼🌼

RATTLESNAKE LAKE

Checklist: 13.2 miles, Out & Back; dirt and gravel railroad grade, dirt trail
Duration: 2–4 hours
Hill factor: one steep hill then easy grade
Skill level: beginner
Season: all year
Map: North Bend Ranger District map
Ownership: public, some private spots
User density: medium; bicyclists, pedestrians, equestrians
Hazards: vertigo from the trestles, snow in winter

Prelude

Several waterfalls cascade down the forested banks above the old Milwaukee Railroad grade, adding a sparkle and romance to this ride. This is an easy ride because of the gradual grade of the old railroad bed. For more information about conditions and the possibility of permits call the the Iron Horse State Park at (509) 656-2230.

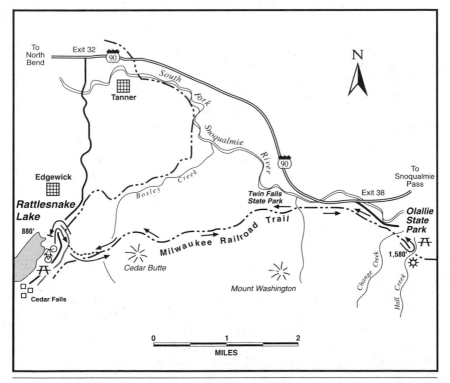

Riding through a cut near Rattlesnake Lake

To get there

Drive east on Interstate 90 to Exit 32. From I-90 drive 3.1 miles to Rattlesnake Lake. From the interstate, turn right onto 436th Ave. S.E. This soon becomes Cedar Falls Road S.E. Stay on Cedar Falls Road all the way to Rattlesnake Lake on the right. Park in the lots next to the lake.

The ride

From the small parking area next to Rattlesnake Lake, pedal back toward I-90 on Cedar Falls Road. At **.3 mile**, turn right onto a gravel road. Just as the road takes a sharp right-hand turn, **.6 mile**, find the narrow trail that exits from the road toward the east. The trail parallels a fence that guards Seattle's watershed. The trail descends for a short pitch. At **.9 mile**, the trail becomes more of a road. At **1 mile**, after a short hill, reach the Milwaukee Railroad Trail. Turn left onto the grade, gradually pedaling up hill. At **2.2 miles**, cross a short trestle over a stream. A delicate waterfall tosses mist into the air on wet days. At **3.5 miles**, cross another trestle with views of a second waterfall on the right. Various roads spur off the main railroad grade: ignore them all. At **4.8 miles**, pass a small transformer station. At **5.5 miles**, bypass a road that cuts down to the left to Olallie State Park. Continue straight up the railroad grade. At **6.3 miles**, cross a long trestle—a beautiful spot to stop for lunch. At **6.5 miles**, cross another trestle that has degenerated into wood planks—be careful. At **6.6 miles**, reach a trestle that washed out several years ago. When you are done staring at the gaping hole, retrace your steps, making the ride **13.2 miles**.

Addition

If you prefer two shots of mountain biking in the morning, you can double the distance by beginning the ride in North Bend. From North Bend, ride out North Bend Way to the intersection of S.E. Tenor Road and North Bend Way, **2.4 miles**. Find the railroad grade that exits from this intersection to the southeast. Ride out the grade to the **7.2-mile mark**, where you meet a paved road near Rattlesnake Lake. Turn left on the road, ride about one-quarter mile, and find the trail at the .6-mile mark of the ride, **7.4 miles**. This Out & Back addition adds 14.8 miles onto the ride.

Ride 6 ✿✿✿

HUMPBACK MOUNTAIN

Checklist: 27.2 miles, Out & Back; wide dirt and gravel trail
Duration: 3–5 hours
Hill factor: steep hill for first mile, then easy grade
Skill level: beginner
Season: spring, summer, fall
Map: North Bend Ranger District map
Ownership: public
User density: medium; bicyclists, hikers, equestrians
Hazards: vertigo from the trestles

Prelude

This ride, along the old railroad grade from Olallie State Park to the Snoqualmie Tunnel, is easy and fun despite the distance and one very tough hill up the first mile. From the trail's perch above the Interstate 90 corridor, great views abound of the South Fork of the Snoqualmie River valley. For more information about conditions and the possibility of permits call the Iron Horse State Park at (509) 656-2230.

To get there

Drive east on Interstate 90 to Exit 38. Turn right at the bottom of the ramp, drive .8 mile, and pull into the gravel parking area at Olallie State Park on the left.

Coasting through an avalanche shed along the railroad grade

The ride

From the Olallie State Park parking area, ride out to the main road and turn left (east). Ride about **60 yards** up the road and take a right up the gated, dirt road. At **.25 mile**, turn left at the intersection. Climb steadily up the rough road to a T at **.6 mile**— turn left. Stay on the main road to **.8 mile**. Take a sharp right, walking the short distance to the railroad grade, **.85 mile**. From the Hall Creek Bridge that's washed out, pedal up the slight grade. At **2.4 miles**, pass through a gate, then bypass a dirt road before passing through another gate. Continue up the railroad grade. At **4.4 miles**, pass by the trail to McClellan Butte. At **9 miles**, cross a high trestle.

The trail edges around the mass of Humpback Mountain on the right. Pass through a snow shed at **11.7 miles**. At **11.9 miles**, bypass the trail to Annette Lake, and continue up the railroad grade. At **13.6 miles**, reach the Snoqualmie Tunnel. From here, turn around and retrace your steps back to Olallie for a total of **27.2 miles**.

Additions

For those with lots of ambition, this railroad trail can be ridden from Duvall (see rides 5, 7, 11, and 12) all the way to Idaho. See *Washington's Rail-Trails*, by Fred Wert.

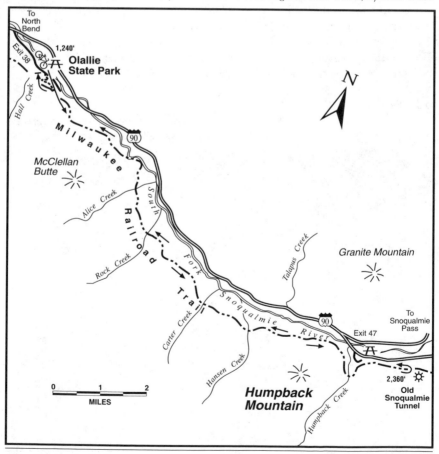

Ride 7 ✿✿✿

ANNETTE LAKE TRAIL TO EASTON

Checklist: 22.9 miles, One Way; dirt and gravel railroad grade, dirt trail
Duration: 4–7 hours
Hill factor: easy downhill grade except for walk up Annette Lake Trail
Skill level: first mile expert, rest intermediate
Season: summer, early fall
Map: North Bend Ranger District
Ownership: public, private
User density: medium; bicyclists, pedestrians, equestrians
Hazards: spooked in the Snoqualmie Tunnel

Prelude

After winding through the forest up the steep and rooted (mostly unridable) Annette Lake Trail, the gradual railroad grade is a welcome sight. Unfortunately, the centerpiece of this ride—the two-and-one-half-mile, perfectly straight Snoqualmie Tunnel—is officially closed, probably due to an insurance company. But the bothersome fence across the opening can allow for the passage of bicycles. If you do ride through the tunnel—at your own risk, of course—use caution. On the way through, you will come to a new meaning of the word darkness, so bring a bike light. Carry extra clothes and wear wool socks since the tunnel can be cold, with a slight breeze and two to four inches of water covering much of the trail. For more information on conditions and the possibility of permits call the the Iron Horse State Park at (509) 656-2230.

To get there

From Seattle, take Interstate 90 to Exit 47, the Denny Creek/Asahel-Curtis Exit. At the end of the freeway ramp, turn right. Take the next left, onto a dirt road toward the Annette Lake Trailhead. Drive about one-quarter mile, and find the trailhead parking lot on the right. Be sure to have a car waiting for you in Easton.

The ride

From the trailhead, begin the pedal and push up the Annette Lake Trail, #1019. At **.25 mile**, cross a bridge. At **.4 miles**, the trail reaches an old road: find the Annette Lake Trail on the opposite side of the road and continue up the trail.

The trail reaches the old Milwaukee Railroad grade at **.9 mile**. Turn left onto the wide, gravel grade. At **2.6 miles**, reach the the Snoqualmie Tunnel. A gate blocks the entrance. From just inside the gate, look for the tiny pinpoint of light at the other end of the tunnel, two-and-one-half miles away. Puddles scatter the route through the tunnel and this combined with a slight breeze make the way chilly. Emerge from the end of the tunnel at **5 miles**. At **5.2 miles**, pass Hyak. From here, the rest of the way is slightly downhill. At **6 miles**, pedal above the shores of Keechelus Lake.

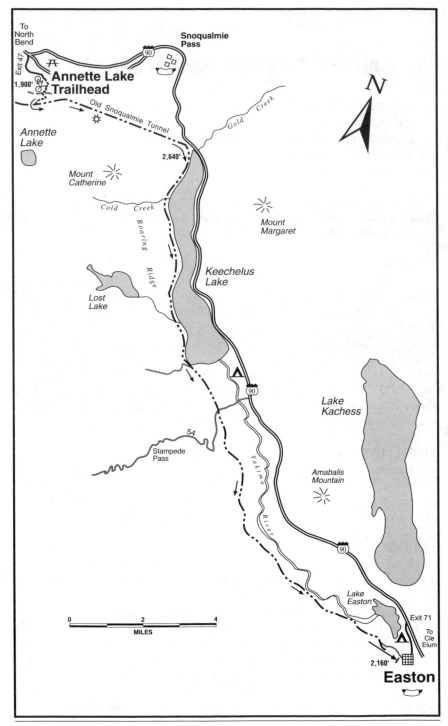

At **8.1 miles**, still above the shores of Keechelus Lake, pass through an avalanche shed. At **11.7 miles**, cross the Moss Lake Road. Continue along the railroad grade which is flat, wide, and nicely packed. At **13.3 miles**, cross the Stampede Pass Road. Ride through another avalanche shed at **15.5 miles**. A number of logging roads spur off the trail—stay on the main railroad grade. At **19.8 miles**, pass through the Iron Horse State Park boundary. Continue down the same grade which is now a used dirt road. Shortly, the dirt road begins paralleling a second railroad grade which still has tracks. At **20.4**

Into the darkness of the Snoqualmie Tunnel

miles, the road turns off to the right and crosses the railroad tracks. Take this right turn. Just across the rails, turn left and follow the tracks. Ride beside these railroad tracks, past Lake Easton. At **22 miles**, cruise through another short tunnel. Near the end of Lake Easton, at **22.3 miles**, the grade meets a road. At **22.4 miles**, reach the dam that creates Lake Easton. Just beyond the dam, bear to the left on a dirt road, crossing the tracks. Stay to the left side of the building with the fence around it. At **22.9 miles**, enter Easton.

If you parked at Lake Easton State Park, turn left and ride about 1 mile farther, on paved roads, to the park.

Ride 8 ✿ ✿ ✿ ✿

WINDY PASS

Checklist: 11.5 miles, Loop; dirt and gravel roads, dirt trails
Duration: 2–4 hours
Hill factor: long, steep, difficult climbs and descents
Skill level: advanced
Season: summer, early fall
Map: Green Trails Snoqualmie Pass
Ownership: public, private
User density: medium; hikers, bicyclists, vehicles on most parts
Hazards: cars, steep descents, rough trails

Prelude

This ride is demanding both physically and technically. The strenuous climbs and rough trail provide ample opportunity to push those limits. But the wonderful forests and awesome Cascade mountain views make it worthwhile. For cyclists who want even more adventure, lots of exploration is possible on the many other trails and roads that weave through the area.

Taking in the Cascades on a blustery day

To get there

Take Interstate 90 to the summit of Snoqualmie Pass. Take Exit 53. Turn right off the ramp, then left (east) toward Ski Acres. Pass the primary Ski Acres parking lot, continuing down to the Ski Acres Cross-Country and Mountain Bike Center, 1.4 miles from I-90. Park in the Mountain Bike Center lot.

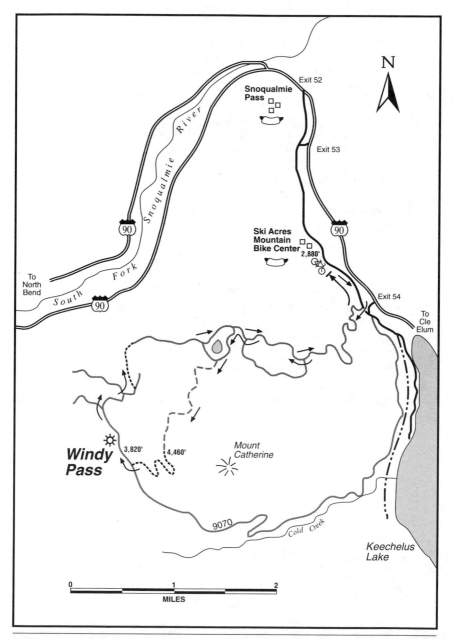

The ride

From the parking lot, ride back out to the road and turn right. Ride **.6 mile**, and, just before Hyak, turn right up a steep dirt road. Ride up the main road, ignoring spurs, until reaching Grand Junction, a five-way intersection, at **3.1 miles**.

From Grand Junction, stand facing the large, wood area map and then proceed down the road to the right. The road bears around to the left, then to the right as you pass the lake at **3.4 miles**. At **3.6 miles**, the road forks: take the left fork up the hill. When the road forks again at **3.9 miles**, take the left fork up a rocky, primitive road. After the steep hill, the way becomes more trail than road, but it is still rather wide. At **4.1 miles**, the trail divides: take the left fork onto trail #18.

From this point, the primitive jeep trail climbs steadily up to the top of Windy Pass at **5.1 miles**. **Whoa**, there are a few tricky spots, but use your best instincts to follow the trail which becomes single-track near the top. From here the trail switchbacks steeply downward. Due to erosion on a poorly built trail, most of the next quarter-mile should be walked until the trail is re-routed.

At **5.4 miles**, the trail arrives at a T at a dirt road. If you turn left, it's an all-out (huge descent) ride back to the parking lot; instead, turn right and climb a short bit to **5.5 miles** where the road passes the Pacific Crest Trail (PCT). Continue up the main gravel road. When the road divides at **5.6 miles**, take the right fork. At **6 miles**, as you pass a tiny pond, again take the right fork, staying on the main road. From the top there are some great views of the Cascades. Just past the lake, bypass a road that exits to the right. At **6.3 miles**—descending quickly—ignore a road off to left; again at **6.7 miles** ignore a road to the left. Then at **6.75 miles**, just past a short bridge, the road divides again. This time take the more primitive fork down to the left. This is a rocky descent. This road becomes a single track that hasn't been fully cleared. At **7.1 miles**, the trail arrives at a rough gravel road next a power-line tower. At **7.3 miles**, the PCT enters from right, and the road is actually PCT for a short way. Stay on main road as it drops quickly. The PCT exits to left at **7.5 miles**. The descent ends and the road tilts up. As you climb the hill, there are several roads that exit—stay on the main road. It's a tough climb. At **8.1 miles**, the road tops out and bends right. Reach Grand Junction at **8.4 miles**. From here, retrace your steps down the dirt road and back to the Ski Acres Mountain Bike Center at **11.5 miles**.

Ride 9 ✿ ✿ ✿ ✿ ✿

KACHESS RIDGE

Checklist: 18.6 miles, Loop; dirt trails, dirt roads
Duration: 4–7 hours
Hill factor: extremely steep grades, much walking
Skill level: expert
Season: summer, early fall
Map: Green Trails Kachess Lake
Ownership: public
User density: medium to light; hikers, equestrians, bicyclists
Hazards: extreme riding

Prelude

This is the most difficult ride in this book: the steep grades combined with the rooted, rocky, and narrow trail challenges even the highly skilled rider. I include Kachess Ridge, however, because it enters the primitive area between Kachess Lake and Cle Elum Lake, a pristine, rugged, alpine ridge.

To get there

From Seattle, drive east on Interstate 90 to Exit 70. Turn left, crossing I-90, then immediately turn left again toward Kachess Dam Road. Take the third right turn (.6 mile). Drive one-quarter mile further and park on the right under the power lines.

Starting up the Kachess Ridge Trail

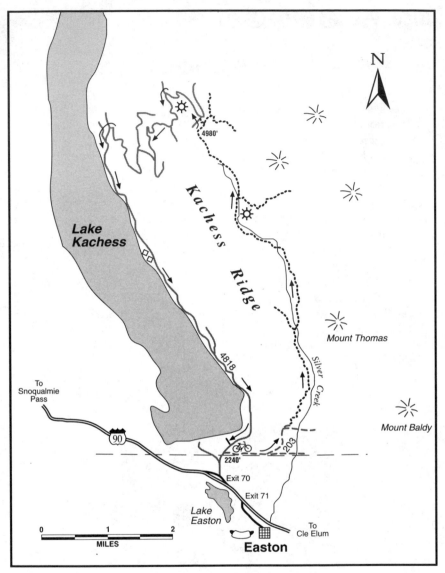

The ride

From the road that crosses under the power lines, turn right, following the power lines southeast. Ride along the power-line access road to a fork at **.7 mile**. Turn left, following the sign toward Kachess Ridge Trail. At **1.25 miles**, the road divides again. Again take the left fork toward the Kachess Ridge Trail. One hundred yards farther, the dirt road ends and the trail begins.

Most riders will have to walk the next **1.25 miles**. Ride and walk the trail as it winds and switchbacks steeply upward. At **2.25 miles**, the trail forks. Switchback up to the right (the trail to the left leads to a lookout). The trail meets Silver Creek at **2.5 miles**,

Walking after the early vigor has dissipated

then levels slightly at **3 miles**. Although the way has leveled somewhat, roots across the trail make the riding very difficult. At **3.2 miles**, the trail divides: take the right fork that crosses Silver Creek.

The next mile is perhaps the best of the entire journey—beautiful meadows combined with numerous stream crossings and alpine views up toward Thomas Mountain and West Peak. By **5 miles**, however, the trail has become steeper and much more technical. At **5.9 miles**, the trail divides. Take the left fork, staying on the Kachess Ridge Trail. The trail continues up a wide bowl-like valley, edging above the tree line. The riding is strenuous and technical.

Reach a saddle at **7 miles**. A huge rock spire stands up to the left. Long views are available on a clear day. From the top, drop precipitously down—walking may be necessary. At **7.4 miles**, find a faint trail on the left that weaves up the steep bank toward a logging road. Leave the main trail and scramble up the bank. **Whoa**, this is an easy turn to miss and the scramble is difficult.

At **7.6 miles**, reach the logging road. The hard part is over; ride roads the rest of the way. Taking the road, turn right and then immediately left. From here, whenever the road divides, take the downhill fork. At **8.5 miles**, turn down to the left. At **9.5 miles**, turn down to the right. At **10.5 miles**, turn down to the right. At **11 miles**, turn left. At **12.2 miles**, turn down to the left. At **12.5 miles**, turn left again. From here, stay on the obvious main road. At **14.2 miles**, pass Boeing Camp. Bypass a road up to the left at **16.5 miles**. Then at **18.6 miles**, reach the power lines and the car.

Ride 10 ✿ ✿✿✿

TOLT-MACDONALD PARK

Checklist: 4.3 miles, Loop; dirt trails, jeep trails
Duration: 1–2 hours
Hill factor: hilly throughout the entire loop
Skill level: first mile advanced then intermediate
Season: all year
Map: USGS Carnation
Ownership: public, private
User density: medium; equestrians, hikers, bicyclists
Hazards: mud

Prelude

The Tolt-MacDonald Loop begins with a steep, loose single-track climb, but then levels out and ambles around the plateau above Carnation, before plunging back down

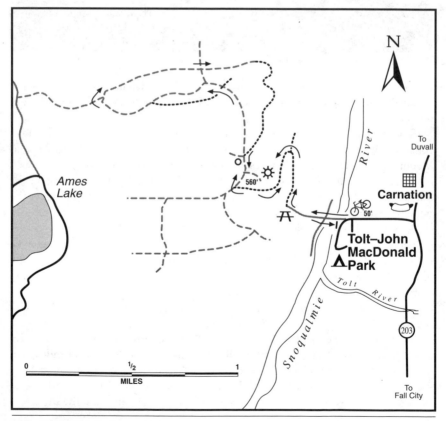

the single track. There's a beautiful view of the Snoqualmie River Valley and the Cascades from the plateau. Once I watched a black bear and two grits cross the trail up on the plateau. It was magic. Unfortunately, development has made this sight rather rare. Tread carefully: when we bicycle into the woods—even near suburban homes—we are in the home of the wildlife.

To get there

Ride or drive to Carnation, a hamlet east of Lake Sammamish on Highway 203 between Duvall and Fall City. Just south of Carnation on Highway 203, find Tolt–John MacDonald Park on the west side of the highway. Drive down the road and park in the lot.

Weaving down the bank into Tolt–MacDonald Park

The ride

From the park, cross the Snoqualmie River on the newly rebuilt suspension bridge. On the opposite bank, take the gravel road that leads away from the river, gradually uphill. About one-quarter mile from the bridge, the gravel road ends at a picnic shelter and a trail begins. The steep trail winds up the bank away from the river. Some sections will have to be walked. At **.5 mile**, turn left at a T in the trail.

At **.85 mile**, the trail reaches a gravel jeep trail: turn right and continue up the hill. (There are several miles of old roads to the left that make for easy, fun riding.) At top of the hill, **1 mile**, bear to the left (if you drop a short distance down to the right, you will find a wonderful view of the Snoqualmie River Valley).

After the left turn, stay on the wide main path. At **1.1 miles**, pass a water tank on the left. Just past the water tank, reach an intersection: continue straight on the main path. At **1.4 miles**, reach another intersection: again, take the center route. Almost immediately, reach another intersection and take a left, away from the main road. At **1.7 miles**, at a right-hand bend in the jeep trail, ignore a faint trail off to the left.

Reach another intersection at **2.1 miles** and turn right. (The left fork drops down to Ames Lake.) At **2.4 miles**, pass a car with the trailer tipped over. At **2.6 miles**, reach an intersection: continue straight. The trail winds and climbs (some scrambling through and around blowdown may be necessary) to the **3.2-mile** mark where it meets the main trail again, one-tenth mile from the watertower. Take a left and retrace your path down to Tolt–John MacDonald Park, **4.3 miles**.

Ride 11 ✸

DUVALL TO CARNATION

Checklist: 8.2 miles, Out & Back; wide dirt and gravel trails
Duration: 1–3 hours
Hill factor: flat
Skill level: beginner
Season: all year
Map: USGS Carnation
Ownership: public
User density: medium; equestrians, bicyclists
Hazards: horse pucky

Prelude

The pasture lands of the lower Snoqualmie Valley between Duvall and Carnation are lovely. A rural, low-tech feel can still be found in King County. The railroad grade between the two towns is being converted into a multi-use trail. This is an easy, flat ride.

To get there

Take Highway 520 to its terminus in Redmond. Cross Highway 202, and take Avondale Road all the way to the Woodinville–Duvall Road. Turn right (east) and drive into Duvall. In Duvall, turn right onto Highway 203 and drive 5.5 miles to a small dirt parking area on the right. A small sign says, "Public Hunting."

Photo by M. Angela Castañeda

Gliding along the railroad corridor toward Carnation

The ride

Beginning from the parking area, ride up to the railroad grade and turn left. Pedal along the trail, crossing cement bridges at **.2 mile**, **.9 mile**, **1.1 miles**, and **1.2 miles**. Whew. The trail angles across a wide field, and then crosses another bridge at **1.7 miles**.

Whoa, at **2.1 miles**, the trail crosses Highway 203, so ride with care. The trail bypasses several roads. At **4 miles**, reach a bridge across the Tolt River. Just beyond the bridge, **4.1 miles**, Remlinger Farms lies off to the left, where you'll find fresh fruit milkshakes among other surprises. From here, turn around and retrace your pedal strokes back to the car at **8.2 miles**.

Additions

• From the beginning of the ride, explore the railroad grade toward Duvall. It's about 5.5 miles to Duvall. About three miles from Duvall, the riding becomes significantly more difficult because the trail has not been completed, forcing you to walk across old beams instead of newly constructed bridges.

• Continuing out the railroad trail from Remlinger Farms, you can connect with the Milwaukee Railroad Trail (page 62).

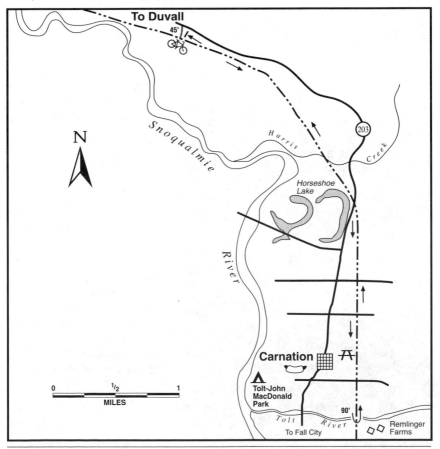

Ride 12 ✿ ✿✿

MILWAUKEE RAILROAD TRAIL—LONG

Checklist: 14 miles, One Way; dirt roads, paved roads, dirt trail
Duration: 1–3 hours
Hill factor: easy, except for a half-mile climb and a short scramble
Skill level: beginner, except for the scramble
Season: all year
Maps: USGS Carnation, USGS Fall City, USGS Snoqualmie
Ownership: public, with some private sections
User density: medium; hikers, bicyclists, vehicles on parts
Hazards: cars on Highway 203, the scramble

Prelude

This is an easy ride up the old Milwaukee Railroad grade, through forests, with pleasant views of the Snoqualmie Valley. Unfortunately this easy ride is disrupted at two difficult spots in the trail, mandating the three-wheel designation. The first is a detour which adds a hill; the second is a difficult scramble—bicycle on shoulder—down a ravine due to a missing bridge. The route has a slight carnival tone since the trail begins near Remlinger Farms and ends at Snoqualmie Falls.

To get there

From the end of Highway 520 in Redmond, take Highway 202 southeast to Fall City. Take two left turns at Fall City to get onto Highway 203. Drive north about 5.5 miles to Carnation. Turn right (east) onto Entwhistle Street, proceed .3 mile, and park at the tiny Nick Loutsis Park on the right. Since this is a One Way ride, remember to park a car near Snoqualmie Falls or else add 14 miles onto the ride, making it 28 miles.

Crossing the bridge over Tokul Creek near Snoqualmie Falls

The ride

From Nick Loutsis Park, find the railroad trail and begin riding south. After **.5 mile**, the trail crosses the Tolt River. Pass Remlinger Farms on the left, **.6 mile**. The way winds easily upward. At **2.75 miles**, the way is blocked by a temporary fence (restricted, keep out) because the grade ahead has slumped a bit. The detour begins here. Take the road to the right and follow it as it drops down to Highway 203, the Carnation–Fall City Road. Reach Highway 203 at **3.8 miles**. Parts of this drive may be private so be sensitive. Turn left onto Highway 203, pedaling toward Fall City. Just as you enter Fall City and cross a bridge, turn left up S.E. 39th Pl., **6.7 miles** (before the Fall City Grill). Around four

Scrambling down the bank at the missing trestle

miles the road becomes dirt and begins climbing up to the railroad grade. At **7.7 miles**, the road seems to divide: continue up and to the right. At **7.9 miles**, the dirt road meets the railroad grade (end of detour). Turn right onto the railroad grade. (The detour adds 2.2 miles to the trip. If the grade is ever repaired, ride up the railroad the entire way and subtract 2.2 miles for the rest of the route.) Ride through several squat gates, then reach a river with no bridge at **9.1 miles**. At this point you will discover a precipitous drop down to the small creek and a long scramble back up to the trail on the opposite side. **Whoa**, this is a dangerous spot, which requires you to carry your bicycle on your shoulder while you climb. At **11.2 miles**, Mount Si looms ahead as the trail bends around to the left. At **11.7 miles**, cross a high bridge above Tokul Creek. This is a wonderful place to stop for a moment and take in the views of the valley and the creek far below. At **12.7 miles**, cross through a short tunnel. Ride about 100 yards farther, and find a trail on the left—**12.9 miles**—that leads to a paved road. Turn left and ride to the intersection of Tokul Road and S.E. 60th Street, **13.2 miles**. From here, turn left and ride down Tokul Road to Highway 202, where you'll find the lodge above Snoqualmie Falls, **14 miles**.

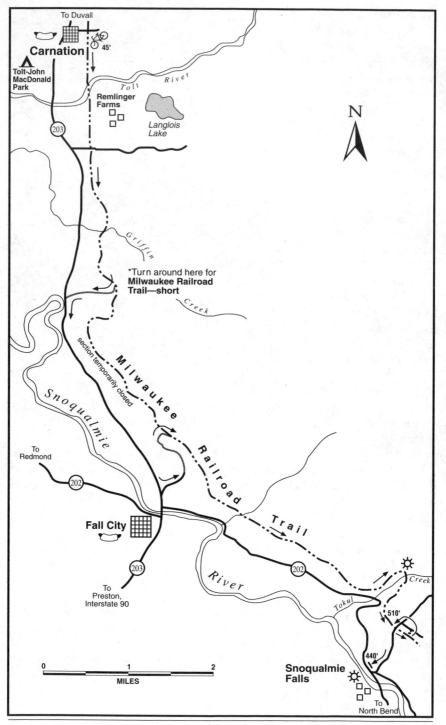

To Duvall

Carnation

45'

Tolt-John
MacDonald
Park

203

Toll *River*

Remlinger
Farms

Langlois
Lake

N

Griffin

*Turn around here for
**Milwaukee Railroad
Trail—short**

Creek

section temporarily closed

Milwaukee

Railroad

Snoqualmie

To
Redmond

202

Trail

Fall City

203

To
Preston,
Interstate 90

River

202

Tokul

Creek

510'

440'

**Snoqualmie
Falls**

To
North Bend

0   1   2
MILES

Ride 13 ✺

MILWAUKEE RAILROAD TRAIL—SHORT

Checklist: 5 miles, Out & Back; dirt and gravel roads
Duration: 1–2 hours
Hill factor: easy climb up the railroad grade
Skill level: beginner
Season: all year
Maps: USGS Fall City, USGS Carnation
Ownership: public
User density: medium; equestrians, hikers, bicyclists

Prelude

This is a short, easy ride for the whole family. The railroad grade provides some nice views of the Snoqualmie Valley as it winds up through foothill forests.

To get there

From Redmond, take Highway 202 southeast to Fall City. Take two left turns at Fall City to get onto Highway 203. Drive north about 5.5 miles to Carnation. Turn right onto Entwhistle Street, proceed .3 mile, and park at Nick Loutsis Park on the right.

The ride

From the park, find the railroad trail and ride south. After **.5 mile**, the trail crosses the Tolt River. Pass Remlinger Farms on the left, **.6 mile**. The way winds easily upward. Bypass several paved and dirt roads. As of early 1993, the trail is blocked at **2.5 miles** due to a small landslide. Turn around here and retrace your steps.

The map

For the map to this ride see the previous page.

Conversation on the Milwaukee Railroad Trail near Fall City

Ride 14 ✽✽✽

MARYMOOR PARK AND BEYOND

Checklist: 23.75 miles, Loop; paved, dirt and gravel trails, and dirt roads
Duration: 3–5 hours
Hill factor: hilly (steep and rolling), some long flat sections, some walking
Skill level: intermediate
Season: all year
Map: USGS Bellevue North
Ownership: public, some private
Use: medium to heavy; equestrians, hikers, bicyclists, rollerbladers
Hazards: getting onto private land by mistake

Prelude

Here's a longer, exploratory ride with plenty of dirt that begins and ends at Marymoor Park. The ride crosses varied terrain, from the paved Sammamish River Trail to technical dirt trails in the Redmond Watershed to the wide gravel path of the Tolt Pipeline Trail. Since it begins near Redmond and travels along a stretch of the Sammamish River Trail, you may be able to ride from home and pick up the ride at any point along the way.

To get there

Pedal or drive to Marymoor Park at the south edge of Redmond, at the eastern end of Highway 520.

The ride

From the Marymoor Park parking lot, ride out toward the entrance. After crossing the Sammamish River find the Sammamish River Trail on the right. Ride north on the trail, past Redmond, to a huge set of power lines that cross the trail at **2.6 miles**. Just past the power lines, **2.7 miles**, find the Puget Power–City of Redmond Trail on the right. Take the dirt trail, right, toward Farrel McWhirter Park. **Whoa**, this is an easy turn to miss, especially after riding along the fast Sammamish River Trail. Shortly, the trail ascends a steep hill through the trees, then exits the trees, **2.8 miles**, and follows the power lines. Cross the Redmond–Woodinville Road, then continue up the steep climb to **3.1 miles,** where the trail levels somewhat. At **4.3 miles**, the trails goes through a muddy area before meeting a paved road. At the road, jog to the left and pick up the paved bicycle path, **4.4 miles**, that climbs the hill. When the trail divides at the top of the hill, take the left fork (gravel) under the power lines and descend down to Avondale Road, **5.3 miles**. Cross Avondale Road and continue east to Ferral McWhirter Park at **5.75 miles**.

At the paved parking circle in Ferral McWhirter Park, take the road up to the left. Climb the steep hill to a T, then turn left on the paved road. Pedal about three blocks, then turn right onto N.E. 116th Street. Pass Redmond Road N.E., then take the next right onto 206th Ave. N.E., **7 miles**. Ride to the end of the road where you'll find a private-property sign under the power lines at **7.3 miles**. The sign says: "Private Property. No Trespassing. Keep Out. Horses and Bicyclists okay." Turn left at the sign onto what is basically a gravel driveway—respect the owners! **At 7.4 miles**, about 70

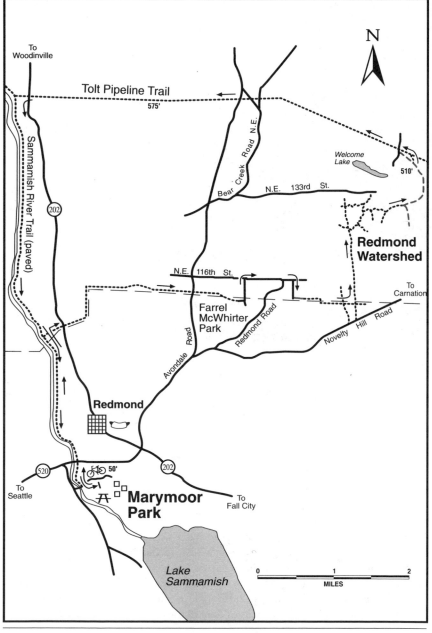

Single track in the Redmond Watershed

yards before the house, find a small grass path on the right that continues to follow the power lines.

The path quickly enters the Redmond Watershed, an 800-acre maze of dirt trails. The trail climbs a hill, hits a fence, then bears around to the right. At **8 miles**, the trail intersects a trail. Don't go right or left; instead, jog to the right about 30 feet and continue on the trail under the power lines. (The trail you have crossed is the Redmond Watershed ride, see page 69.) At **8.2 miles**, climb the short dirt embankment where the power lines intersect a gas pipeline. At this point, turn left and ride along the gas pipeline trail. After several steep ups and downs, climb to a high point at **9.2 miles**. Several trails intersect at the wide dirt circle at the top. Take the trail on the right. The trail climbs for a short way then levels. Stay on the main trail, ignoring spurs. At **9.5 miles**, the trail divides. Stay to the left on the main trail. When the trail divides again at **9.75 miles**, take the right fork, which winds frenetically through the woods. Pass a trail on the right at **9.9 miles** (stay to the left), and ride to the old cedar railroad grade, **10.2 miles**. At the railroad grade, turn left and ride straight down the gradual grade to a fork at **10.6 miles**. Take the left fork (straight). At **11.4 miles**, find a rough, narrow trail on the right. **Whoa**, this is easy to miss.

The trail pops out onto the Tolt Pipeline Trail—wide, loose gravel, straight—at **11.6 miles**. Turn left onto the trail, riding up and down and crossing many roads. At times the Tolt Pipeline is steep (the top is at 15.9 miles). At **16.8 miles**, after a steep downhill, the water pipe is exposed; it actually crosses above a road. Cross the road and find the trail below the pipeline to the left. Walk up the steep, narrow trail to the bluff and continue riding down the pipeline trail. After an incredibly steep downhill, **17.3 miles**, cross another road and ride about one-quarter mile to the Sammamish Valley Trail, **17.7 miles**. Take a left onto the trail. At **23.5 miles**, reach Marymoor Park. Turn left into the park, and pedal one-quarter mile to the car for a total of **23.75 miles**.

Ride 15 ✦✦✦

REDMOND WATERSHED—SHORT

Checklist: 4.5 miles, Loop; dirt trails
Duration: 1–2 hours
Hill factor: many short climbs (some quite steep), some walking
Skill level: advanced
Season: summer, fall
Maps: USGS Bellevue North
Ownership: Redmond, private
User density: extremely high; bicyclists, equestrians, hikers
Hazards: mud, erosion, other users, roots, Novelty Hill Road

Prelude

Mountain bicyclists populate the Redmond Watershed like gum balls in a gum-ball machine. This is a beautiful and excellent place to ride, with tons of technical dirt trails that wind frenetically up and down and around. It's also close and easy to get to. But the watershed is overpopulated with mountain bicyclists. Many cyclists have ridden inappropriately in wet conditions, causing some trail erosion. If it's wet, give the watershed a break and try another ride.

Maneuvering through trees in the Redmond Watershed

To get there

From the intersection of Highway 520 and Highway 202 in Redmond, ride or drive northeast on Avondale Road. After 1.6 miles, bear right onto Novelty Hill Road. Drive 2.4 miles on Novelty Hill Road. Park alongside the road just before or after 218th Ave. N.E. Nearby residents have complained about mountain-biker garbage. Keep this section of Novelty Hill Road clean. In addition, this is an very busy, high-speed road, so use extreme caution when crossing it.

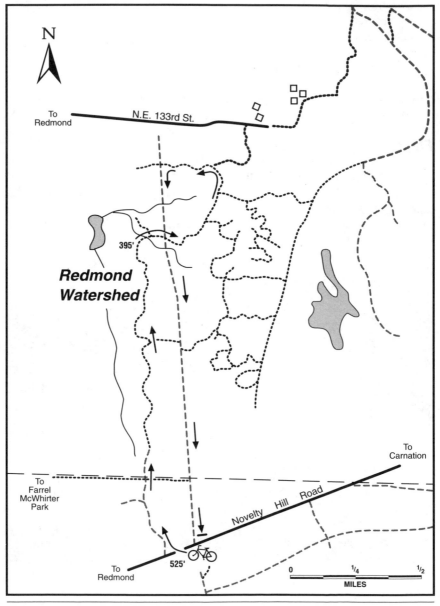

The ride

From the intersection of N.E. Novelty Hill Road and 218th Ave. N.E., ride north on 218th, through the gate and down the dirt road. At **.2 mile**, the road forks: veer to the right. Just around the corner, stay to the right again. Reach a four-way intersection and a set of power lines at **.4 mile**. Continue straight through this intersection. (See page 66 to learn about the trail that parallels the power lines.)

The trail, winding and rooted, becomes more challenging after the power lines. At **1.1 miles**, bypass a trail on the right, continue straight on main trail. The path continues to wind up and down through the dark forest. At **1.8 miles**, just after crossing a stream, arrive at a T in trail. Turn right and ride up a long, tough, gravely hill to a four-way intersec-

Oncoming mud puddle

tion at a flat open area, **1.9 miles**. The open corridor to the right and left is the gas-pipeline right of way. Instead, ride straight across the flat open area to a trail into the woods and continue uphill.

At **2 miles**, reach the top and bear to the left. When the trail divides at **2.2 miles**, take the left fork. At **2.5 miles**, the trail divides again: continue straight on the left fork. At **2.6 miles**, the trail comes to a T: turn left. Pedal a short distance to the gas pipeline, **2.8 miles**. Turn left onto the wide, dirt pipeline trail, ignoring the single track across the pipeline. At **3.1 miles**, after a fast ride down and across a creek and a push up a hill, return to the flat open area described at 1.9 miles.

Do another loop or explore other trails from this point. If you're ready to get back to Novelty Hill Road, continue straight. Immediately from the open flat area the trail drops steeply. There are several steep down-and-ups—some walking will be necessary. At **3.7 miles**, ignore a trail off to right; at **3.8 miles**, ignore a trail off to left. Reach the power lines and continue straight. From the power lines, there's a steep descent that must be walked. Continue along the gas pipeline trail to Novelty Hill Road at **4.5 miles**.

Ride 16 ✿✿✿

REDMOND WATERSHED—LONG

Checklist: 8.1 miles, Loop; dirt trails, dirt roads
Duration: 2–3 hours
Hill factor: many short climbs (some quite steep), some walking
Skill level: advanced
Season: summer, fall
Maps: USGS Bellevue North
Ownership: Redmond, private
User density: extremely high; bicyclists, equestrians, hikers
Hazards: mud, erosion, other users, roots, Novelty Hill Road

Prelude

Most of Western Washington is classified as rain forest. The Redmond Watershed, with its thick canopy and lush undergrowth, proves this true ten out of twelve months each year. Even on the driest days between September and June you are liable to run into puddles and mud bogs and swollen streams around each turn in the trail. Too many bicyclists have been eroding the watershed trails by riding them when they're too wet. If you want a wet, muddy ride, try Novelty Hill (page 75), Lake Desire (page 106), or Tahuya State Forest (page 130).

To get there

From the intersection of Highways 520 and 202 in Redmond, drive northeast on Avondale Road. Travel 3.8 miles, then turn right onto Bear Creek Road N.E. Go one-quarter mile farther, and turn right onto N.E. 133rd Street. Drive to the Laura Ingalls Wilder School at the end of N.E. 133rd Street and park alongside the road.

Treading lightly over a series of roots

The ride

From the Laura Ingalls Wilder School, ride west, back toward Avondale Road. At just **.1 mile**, find a faint trail on the left (opposite the school). A few pedal strokes down the trail, enter the Redmond Watershed. Reach a fork in the trail at **.3 mile**: turn left. Arrive at another fork at **.4 mile**: turn left. When the trail divides again at **.5 mile**, take a left. After a hectic series of hairpin turns and root crossings, reach a T at an old railroad grade, **.8 mile**. Turn left and ride slightly downhill. At **.9 mile**, cross a stream and bear to the left. The trail leaves the watershed at **1.1 miles**.

Reach a mud bog and an intersection at **1.2 miles**. Take a right onto a jeep road and begin a short climb. (The road to the left accesses the Tolt Pipeline; see page 66.) When the trail forks, **1.4 miles**, take the right fork. (The left fork gets you to the same destination and is slightly shorter.) At **2 miles**, the rough jeep trail reaches a T: turn

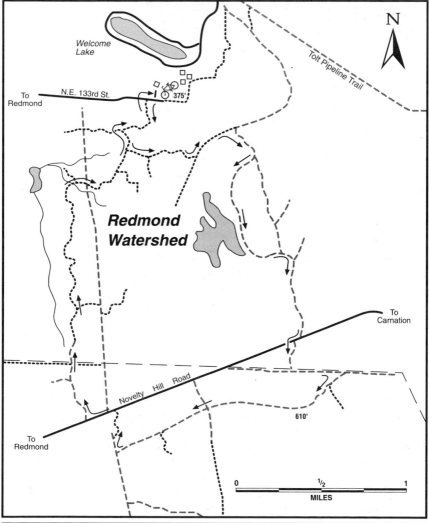

A *peaceful section of the Redmond Watershed Trail*

right. From here, stay on the main road. Reach Novelty Hill Road, **2.75 miles**.

Cross Novelty Hill Road, turn right, then look for a trail that exits the road on the left, **2.8 miles**. Ride down a dark, muddy road to a set of power lines at the **3-mile point**. Turn left onto the power-line road and ride gradually downhill. (This road is part of two rides in *Kissing the Trail*: pages 34, 75.) At **3.3 miles**, the road forks: turn right and ride into the woods away from the power lines. From here, stay on the main trail, ignoring a trail on the left at **3.4 miles**. Reach a four-way intersection at **4.2 miles**: continue straight. At **4.5 miles**, bypass a trail on the left; continue straight. At **4.75 miles**, reach a T at a wide, dirt road. This is the gas-pipeline right of way. Turn right and ride for a short distance to a trail that bears into the woods on the right, **4.9 miles**. This trail winds through the woods to Novelty Hill Road, **5 miles**.

Carefully cross Novelty Hill Road, turn left, then ride down the road to a gated, dirt road (218th Ave. N.E.) on the right, **5.2 miles**. Ride through the gate and down the dirt road. At **5.4 miles**, the road forks: veer to the right. Just around the corner, stay to the right again. Reach a four-way intersection and a set of power lines at **5.6 miles**. Continue straight. (See page 66 to learn about the trail that parallels the power lines.)

The trail, winding and rooted, becomes more challenging. At **6.3 miles**, pass a trail on the right; continue straight on main trail. The path winds up and down through the dark forest. At **7 miles**, just after crossing a stream, arrive at a T in the trail. Turn right and ride up a long, tough, gravely hill to a four-way intersection at a flat open area, **7.1 miles**. The open corridor to the right and left is the gas-pipeline right of way. Ignore it, and ride straight across the flat open area to a trail into the woods and continue uphill.

At **7.2 miles**, reach the top and bear to the left. When the trail divides at **7.4 miles**, take the left fork. At **7.7 miles**, the trail divides again: continue straight (the left fork). At **7.8 miles**, the trail comes to a T: turn right. Pedal a short distance to a road, N.E. 133rd, **8 miles**. Turn right and ride back to the car, **8.1 miles**.

Ride 17 ✺✺

NOVELTY HILL

Checklist: 5 miles, Loop; dirt trails, dirt roads
Duration: 1–2 hours
Hill factor: easy rolling hills
Skill level: beginner
Season: all year
Map: USGS Bellevue North
Ownership: private
User density: medium; equestrains, bicyclists, hikers
Hazards: primordial horse soup, mud

Prelude

This is a pleasant, cruiser ride through wet, forested lands, with no difficult hills. This 800-acre plot is scheduled to be developed into 5,000 units over the next fifteen years—use it while you can. The Last Dirt Trail winds through here (see page 34).

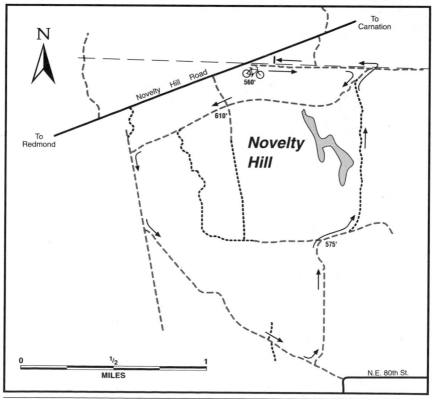

To get there

From the intersection of Highway 520 and Highway 202 in Redmond, ride or drive northeast on Avondale Road. After 1.6 miles, bear right onto Novelty Hill Road. Just as you pass under some power lines, about 4.8 miles from Redmond, pull into a small, informal dirt parking spot on the right side of Novelty Hill Road under the power lines.

The ride

From the south side of Novelty Hill Road, ride up the primitive dirt road under the power lines. At **.3 mile**, bypass a trail on the left that leads to the Redmond Watershed. Continue down the power-line road. After riding **.7 mile**, the road forks: take the sharp right fork away from the power

Autumn riding near Novelty Hill

lines and into the woods. Ride along this primitive road, bypassing a trail to the left at **.9 mile** and a four-way intersection at **1.6 miles**. Stay on the main trail. The dirt road climbs slightly and then drops.

At **2.4 miles**, the dirt road ends at the natural gas–pipeline access road. Turn left here, following the wide dirt road to the south. The pipeline road and the series of short neighborhood trails in the woods on the right provide entertaining riding, but when you spot a road that exits the pipeline road on the left at **2.8 miles**, take it. Ride along this road, passing a road and two trails on the right and a trail on the left. Stay on the main road. When the road divides at **4 miles**, take the left fork (if you come to a paved road, you've gone too far). Ride gradually up the dirt road to the **4.7-mile mark** where the road ends at a T. Turn right and ride several hundred yards to a fork: take the primitive road to the left. At **5.7 miles**, the way meets a road—turn right. Ride along this road until you reach the power lines, **5.9 miles**. Turn left and ride up the power-line road to Novelty Hill Road, **6.6 miles**.

Ride 18 ✿ ✿✿✿

NORTHWEST PASSAGE

Checklist: 6.9 miles, Out & Back; dirt trails, jeep trails
Duration: 1–3 hours
Hill factor: short rolling hills (some steep), several short walks
Skill level: advanced
Season: spring, summer, fall
Maps: USGS Fall City, USGS Bellevue South
Ownership: private property, Washington State DNR
User density: medium; equestrians, bicyclists
Hazards: hidden stumps, other users, mud

Prelude

Here's a fun, winding, narrow single track through forests near Redmond. It passes through a lovely grove of large cedars scheduled to become a golf course in the next few years. Much of the trail is so curvy and overgrown, it's difficult to see far ahead, so keep your speed down and be alert for horses on the trail. If you encounter horses, pull off the trail, talking to the horse and rider as they pass. Help make this trail, section 36, a multi-use park that includes mountain bicyclists: call the King County Council. The Last Dirt Trail winds through here (see page 34).

To get there

From the intersection of Highways 520 and 202 in Redmond, ride or drive east on Highway 202, the Redmond–Fall City Road. After 5.4 miles, turn right on 244th Ave. N.E. Take 244th to N.E. 8th Street, turn left and go .5 mile to the power lines. Park under the power lines.

The ride

From N.E. 8th Street and the power lines, find the trail on the south side of the street. Pedal up the trail, which varies back and forth between single track and jeep trail. The trail parallels a fence for about 50 yards, then bears to the right, back out underneath the power lines. At **.5 mile**, a dirt road cuts back to the left; continue on the main road along the power lines. Several pedal strokes farther, the road divides again; take the main road to the right (the two roads converge again after less than one-quarter mile). Over the next one-quarter mile, several trails and an old road exit to the right and make for interesting exploration. Instead stay on the main road.

At **.9 mile**, five feet after the fifth power-line tower, take the lesser, grassy road on the left, passing under the wires. The trail ducks into the woods and immediately you'll need to change from dark to clear lenses. At **1.1 miles**, the trail divides: the right fork climbs 15 yards up to a small lookout over a large swamp, then ends. Continue straight— the left fork—over roots, through mud pockets and underbrush, and around fallen trees.

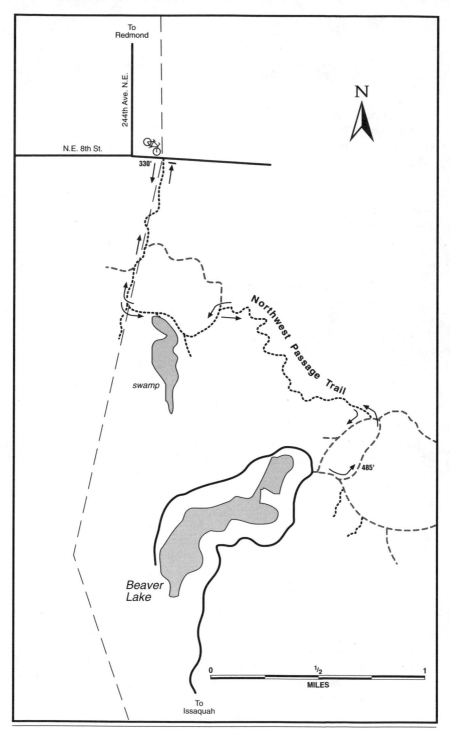

When the trail forks, stay on the main trail to the left (don't take the faint Beaver Dam Trail on the right.)

After **1.6 miles**, the trail widens slightly, then forks again. (The left fork returns you to the power lines in .8 mile, a half-mile from N.E. 8th Street.) Instead, take the right fork and ride quietly into a wonderful old cedar grove. From here, stay on the main trail as it snakes through a lush and wonderful forest, the essence of the Northwest Passage.

At the **3-mile mark**, the Northwest Passage Trail ends at a primitive road (see Beaver Lake East, page 87.). Turn right, riding up a gentle grade. When the road forks at **3.2 miles**, take a left. From here, the road narrows and traverses downhill to another road at **3.4 miles**. To the right you'll see a fence and a paved street. Turn left and ride up the jeep trail. At **3.5 miles**, turn left again on another jeep trail. The jeep trail becomes a single track, and then at **3.9 miles** reaches an intersection: turn left, then, twenty yards further, find the Northwest Passage Trail on the right. Ride back to N.E. 8th Street the same way you came, making the ride **6.9 miles**.

Riding through the majestic forests of the Northwest Passage

Ride 19 ✹ ✹

SAINT EDWARD PARK

Checklist: 2 miles, Loop; dirt trails
Duration: 1 hour
Hill factor: short rolling hills, steep hill to beach
Skill level: intermediate
Season: all year
Map: Saint Edward State Park map
Ownership: public
User density: high; hikers, bicyclists
Hazards: rough trail

Prelude

Although this is a very short ride, you can do more than one circuit to add to the mileage. Saint Edward Park is in a beautiful setting on the forested northeast shore of Lake Washington. Other than the spur trail down to the lake, the trails are fairly flat, but sections of the trail are winding and quite technical. Some of these trails were built by the Backcountry Bicycle Trails Club, and more trails are planned.

To get there

From Seattle, take Lake City Way (Highway 522) to Kenmore. Turn right onto Juanita Dr., then watch for St. Edward Park on the right. Or from Interstate 405, take Exit 20A. Turn west onto N.E. 116th Street (becomes Juanita Dr.). After 3 miles, find St. Edward Park on the left. Drive into the park, take the second left, and park above the playfield.

Climbing a hill above Lake Washington

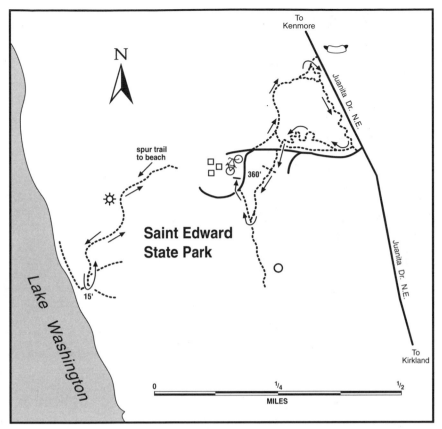

The ride

From the parking area above the playfield, pedal back toward the main road. At the first intersection—**30 yards**—find the trail across the road. Ride down the main trail, bypassing spurs to the right at **.2 mile** and **.5 mile**. At **.6 mile**, just before Juanita Drive, turn right. When the trail divides after a few pedal strokes, turn left. Follow the winding trail to **.9 mile**. Turn right before reaching the road into Saint Edward Park. Just past this turn, the trail forks: take the right fork. At **1.5 miles**, the trail reaches a T. Turn left and ride 20 yards to the road. On the opposite side of the road, find a faint trail that winds through the woods above the playing field. Do not turn off this trail. At **1.8 miles**, reach a wide, heavily used trail—turn right. Ride down the hill, and find the parking lot, **2 miles**.

Spur trail to the beach

From the west side of the seminary building, find a wide trail that descends from the expansive lawn. The trail winds down through a forest with wonderful views of Lake Washington. At **.6 mile** from the seminary, reach the beach. Trails exit in several directions, but they are closed to bicycles. Turn around, retracing your steps up the steep climb back to the buildings. This Out & Back spur adds **1.2 miles** to the ride.

Ride 20 ✸ ✸ ✸

GRAND RIDGE—SHORT

Checklist: 4.9 miles, Loop; dirt trails
Duration: 1–2 hours
Hill factor: Steep up and down
Skill level: advanced
Season: all year
Maps: USGS Fall City, USGS Bellevue South
Ownership: private
User density: medium; hikers, bicyclists
Hazards: rough trails, mud

Prelude

The riding at Grand Ridge varies from delicate alpine-like trails to mud central on pre–real estate development jeep roads. At times the trail is smooth, at times rocky; some stretches of trail pass under power lines, others crisscross through the woods. Much of the area is scheduled for development. The Last Dirt Trail winds through Grand Ridge Trail system (see page 34).

To get there

Drive east on Interstate 90 past Issaquah to Exit 20, the High Point Exit. Take the first left, drive under the freeway, and park in the small dirt parking area on the left.

Near the trailhead at Grand Ridge

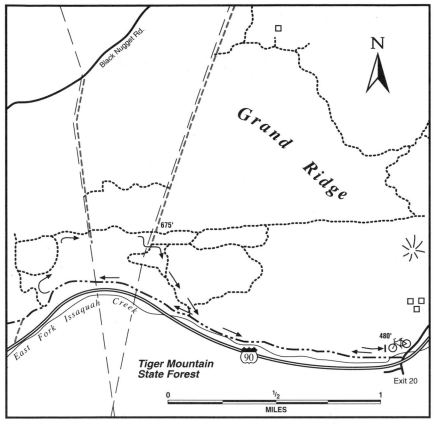

The ride

Beginning from the parking area, walk carefully over the old bridge above the East Fork of Issaquah Creek. Pedal down the wide dirt railroad grade that descends slightly. Bypass a single-track trail up to the right at **1.1 miles**; continue down the railroad grade. At **1.9 miles**, find a narrow trail up to the right. Immediately the trail begins a steep climb up loose dirt and rock. Part of this climb may have to be walked. The way levels around **2.2 miles**; the most difficult climb of this route is complete.

At **2.3 miles**, the trail divides: take the right fork. Begin climbing again but up a better riding surface. The trail levels, then reaches a T at **2.7 miles**. Take a right onto a slightly wider trail. At **2.9 miles**, drop down the hill to a four-way intersection under a set of power lines. Continue straight, pedaling up the steep hill. The trail re-enters the woods and continues climbing.

At **3.2 miles**, arrive at a four-way intersection at a second, more substantial, set of power lines. Instead of continuing straight, turn right; then quickly turn left, away from the power lines. At **3.3 miles**, reach a fork: turn right. The trail drops rapidly. At **3.5 miles**, the trail forks again: take the left fork, downhill. At **3.8 miles**, the trail divides just above the railroad grade: take a right, and then a left when you reach the railroad grade. Ride back to the small parking area, making the ride **4.9 miles**.

Ride 21 ❋❋❋❋

GRAND RIDGE—LONG

Checklist: 9 miles, Loop; dirt trails
Duration: 2–4 hours
Hill factor: Steep up and down
Skill level: advanced
Season: all year
Maps: USGS Fall City, USGS Bellevue South
Ownership: private
User density: medium; hikers, bicyclists
Hazards: rough trails, mud

Prelude

The long Grand Ridge loop is similar to the shorter ride (page 82) in that the riding varies from delicate alpine-like trails to mud-city jeep roads. The entire area will be developed sometime during the next ten years, probably much sooner, so ride it now. But don't go riding at Grand Ridge if you don't want to get muddy. The Last Dirt Trail winds through the Grand Ridge Trail system (see page 34).

Ducking blowdown at Grand Ridge

To get there

Drive east on Interstate 90 past Issaquah to Exit 20, the High Point Exit. Take the first left, drive under the freeway, and park immediately in the small dirt parking area on the left.

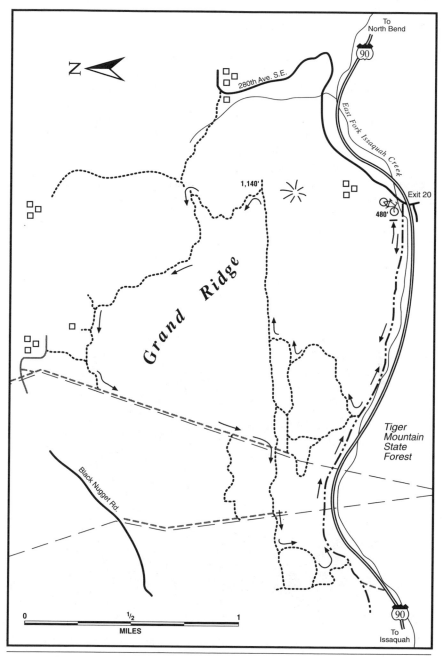

The ride

Beginning from the parking area, walk carefully over the old bridge above the East Fork of Issaquah Creek. Pedal down the wide dirt railroad grade that descends slightly. At **1.1 miles**, take the single-track trail up to the right. The trail forks again almost immediately, take a right. Ride up the long, quite steep hill to a fork at **2 miles**: take the sharp right fork. **Whoa**, this is a easy turn to miss. From this intersection the trail winds frenetically through the trees and thick undergrowth to a T at a trail, **2.2 miles**.

From the T, turn right. The trail becomes quite steep at **2.3 miles**, probably mandating a push. Reach the top of the Grand Ridge Trail system at **2.9 miles**. About 10 yards before the top, find a trail off to the left. The trail drops rapidly to a fork at **3.3 miles**. Take the sharp, left fork; begin climbing. After ascending a ways, the trail drops down the incredibly rocky flat-tire trail. At **4.3 miles**, the trail divides: take the left fork. When the trail forks at **4.4 miles**, go left. Take the left fork again at **4.7 miles**. At **4.8 miles**, the trail reaches a road under the power lines—turn left.

Ride under the power lines, bypassing a trail on the right at **5.7 miles**, to a four-way intersection at the **5.9-mile mark**. Take a right, and ride back into the woods. At **6.2 miles**, the trail emerges from the trees and drops to a four-way intersection at a second, smaller set of power lines. Continue straight through this intersection, up the hill and back into the woods. At **6.3 miles**, the trail forks: turn left. When the trail arrives at a T, **6.8 miles**, turn left.

From the T, the trail descends quickly down a rough trail to a junction with the railroad grade, **7.1 miles**. Turn left onto the wide, gradually uphill road. At **9 miles**, reach the small parking area.

Night riding near Grand Ridge

Ride 22 ✸✸

BEAVER LAKE EAST

Checklist: 4 miles, Loop; dirt trails, jeep trails
Duration: 1 hour
Hill factor: slight rolling hills, no difficult climbs
Skill level: beginner
Season: all year
Map: USGS Fall City
Ownership: private
User density: medium; equestrians, hikers, bicyclists
Hazards: bulldozers, nettles, mud

Prelude

Some of the most wild and crazy real estate development is occurring on the outskirts of Issaquah. This ride may be the first one that development eliminates from *Kissing the Trail*. But Beaver Lake is perhaps the best area for the beginner to check out trail riding for the first time: the trails are easy, the hills are few, and the loop is short. The Last Dirt Trail winds through this area (see page 34); it's a beautiful area that should have been a county park.

To get there

From Exit 17 off Interstate 90 in Issaquah, take Lake Sammamish Parkway north. Take the first right onto the Issaquah–Pine Lake Road. Turn right again onto the Issaquah–Fall City Road. After several miles take the left fork onto S.E. Duthie Hill Road. Turn left onto 266 Ave. S.E. This road quickly becomes S.E. 27th Street. Then turn right onto 261 Ave. S.E. Park in the turn-around at the end of the cul-de-sac.

The ride

Ride out the trail that originates from the turn-around, past a "No Motor Vehicles" sign. When you reach a four-way intersection at **.25 mile**, take the center trail (not straight and not sharp left). **Whoa**, this is a tricky turn because it looks more like two trails that swing close together than an intersection. To take the center trail, turn left for ten feet, then right. From the intersection, the trail winds through the woods, reaching a jeep trail at the **.65-mile point**. Turn left onto the jeep trail. The jeep trail forks immediately: take the left fork. At **.8 mile**, just before a fence, turn right onto a narrow trail. The trail widens, then at **1 mile** take the right fork.

At **1.2 miles**, pass the Northwest Passage trail (see page 77) on the left. Stay on the main road. When the jeep trail divides at **1.25 miles**, turn left, dropping down to a low point in the trail which is often muddy. Continue straight at **1.8 and 1.9 miles**, ignoring a road and a trail up to the right. A few pedal strokes farther, ignore a trail off to the left and then a road on the right. Stay on the main jeep trail.

Maneuvering around a puddle near Beaver Lake

At **2.2 miles**, the jeep trail forks. Take a left. Again, stay on the main jeep trail, ignoring the trails to the right and left, to the **2.5-mile mark** where the trail runs into a clearing and connects with a jeep trail that cuts back to the right. Take the hard right fork. Ride along the jeep trail, ignoring slight trails off to either side. At **3 miles**, pass a barn off to the left. The trail forks at **3.25 miles**: take a left. Then at **3.5 miles**, turn left (away from the main jeep trail) onto a narrow trail. At **3.75 miles**, reach the four-way intersection near the beginning of the ride. From here, you can ride one-quarter mile to the parking area, **4 miles**.

Exploration addition

Throughout the loop there are numerous trails and jeep roads that provide great exploration. The route described is a large loop, and many of the spur trails bisect the circle. In addition to those trails, another area, known by some as the Spider Web, can be reached from the four-way intersection. These trails are short but somewhat more challenging than the main Beaver Lake ride. From the parking area, ride out the trail

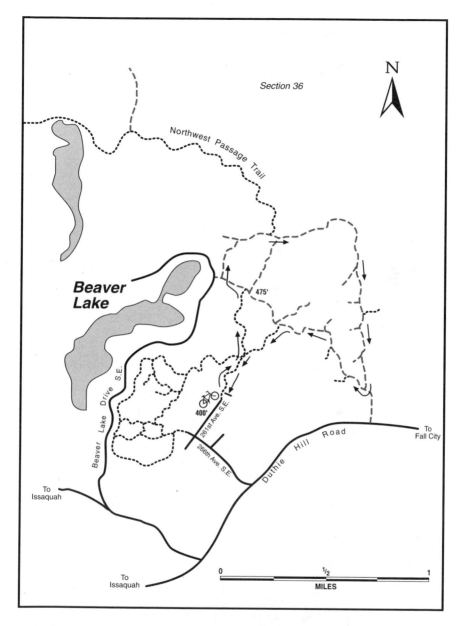

to the four-way intersection, **.25 miles**. Hang a sharp left. Ride the narrow, dirt trail to a fork at the **.75-mile mark** on the top of a small ridge. Take the right fork that treads the ridgetop. To return to the .75-mile point, take the next four left turns: **.9, .92, 1, and 1.02 miles**. Return to the .75-mile point at **1.05 miles**. Then backtrack the .75 mile to the parking area, making the addition **1.8 miles** long. The real exploration and fun begins by taking a right at some point and riding into the web of trails beyond.

Ride 23 🏵 🏵 🏵 🏵

EAST COUGAR MOUNTAIN

Checklist: 4.6 miles, Loop; dirt trails, jeep trails
Duration: 1–4 hours
Hill factor: steep up and down entire ride
Skill level: advanced
Season: all year
Map: USGS Bellevue South
Ownership: private
User density: medium; bicyclists, hikers
Hazards: rough trail

Prelude

Cougar Mountain is a special place: a huge, beautiful park close to the urban centers of Bellevue and Seattle. Early in this century, logging and mining companies completely denuded Cougar, leaving roads, railroad grades, and few trees. But over the years the mountain has rebounded to the point that it's now called a "wildland" park. Until 1988, mountain bikes shared the trails and dirt roads on Cougar with pedestrians and equestrians. The area is particularly suited to mountain biking because the old roads and

Churning and sweating up a trail on Cougar Mountain

railroad grades are wide and moderately sloped. Cougar is one of the best mountain biking areas in western Washington. Unfortunately, in 1988 Cougar was designated a wildland park, a designation that, King County Parks say, excludes bicycles. Mountain bicyclists have worked hard to get King County to change the anti-bike interpretation, with no success. This ride gives you a taste of the beauty and ridability of Cougar without crossing into the park. If you enjoy this ride and believe more of Cougar should be open to mountain bikes, write your King County Council member. This ride is steep at times, and irregularities in the old roads make the riding quite technical.

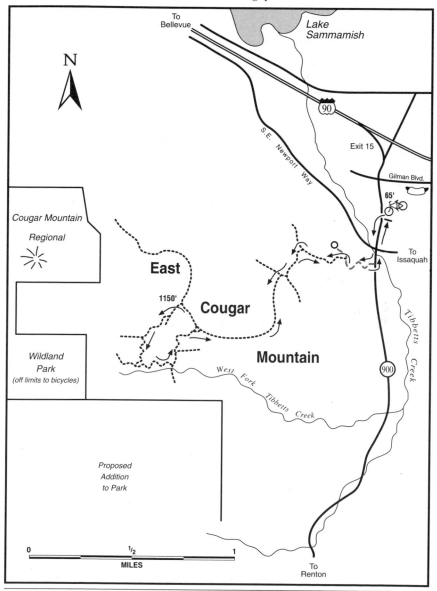

To get there

Drive or ride to Exit 15 on Interstate 90. Go west on State Rte. 900 for about one-quarter-mile to the Park-and-Ride lot on the left. Park here.

The ride

From the Park-and-Ride lot, ride to State Rte. 900 and turn left, away from I-90. At **.2 mile**, cross Newport Way. Continue up State Rte. 900. At **.3 mile**, turn right onto the first paved road after Newport Way. This road is quite steep and a shock to the system so early in the ride. The road quickly turns to gravel. At **.4 mile**, reach a wire across the road; continue up. After the wire, the road bends to the right and the hill levels somewhat. At the crest of the hill, **.6 mile**, find an old grassy road that exits left. **Whoa**, this is easy to miss. (If you begin riding downhill, you've gone too far.)

Ride up the rugged old road. Parts may have to be walked due to blowdown and irregularities in the road surface. The trail varies from old road to single track and back. At **.8 mile**, the trail forks: turn left toward the Shangri-La Road. At **1 mile**, the trail divides; take the right fork up the hill. Almost immediately the trail divides again; this time take the left fork. From here the trail traverses up and around the steep hillside. At **1.6 miles**, bypass a road off to the left, and continue up the main road that bears to the right. (That faint road off to the left is the road you will return on.) At **1.7 miles**, stay on main trail, bypassing a lesser spur to the right as the trail bears to the left.

Arrive at top of the ride at Pulper Junction, **2 miles**. The right fork heads toward the Cougar Mountain Regional Wildland Park boundary. Instead, turn left, toward State Rte. 900. At **2.1 miles**, the road forks; take a right toward State Rte. 900. A couple of pedal strokes farther, the road seems to end. Bear to the left and find a single-track trail that continues into the woods. **Whoa**, this is a confusing section. Ride the single track to a fork at **2.25 miles**. Take the lesser trail to the left toward Protector Ridge and State Rte. 900. **Whoa**, this is also an easy turn to miss (don't go up the hill). This narrow trail gradually descends through the woods toward Tibbetts Creek. At **2.5 miles**, the trail reaches a T at the Tibbetts Creek ravine. Turn left, riding down the ridge along a narrow, technical trail that requires several dismounts. At **2.8 miles**, the single track drops down to a road. A sign "To Bear Ridge, Fantastic Erratic" lures you to the right. Instead, turn left. Stay left again at **2.9 miles** when the West Tibbetts Creek Trail spurs off to the right. Do not take this trail to the right: continue down the old road. At **3 miles**, reach an intersection—turn right. A few pedal strokes farther, the road joins the road you came up on. Stay right, retracing your steps. At **3.6 miles**, turn right, then immediately left. At **3.8 miles**, turn down to the right. At **4 miles**, reach the gravel road and turn right. Ride down the road to State Rte. 900 at **4.3 miles**. Turn left on State Rte. 900 and ride back to the Park-and-Ride lot, **4.6 miles**.

Ride 24 ✿✿✿

SQUAK MOUNTAIN

Checklist: 6.5 miles, Loop; dirt trails, dirt roads
Duration: 1–3 hours
Hill factor: steep up and down entire ride
Skill level: advanced
Season: all year
Map: USGS Bellevue South
Ownership: public, short private sections
User density: medium; hikers, bicyclists, equestrians
Hazards: unmaintained trail, logging in sections

Prelude

Squak Mountain, the Issaquah Alp sandwiched between Cougar Mountain and Tiger Mountain, provides a unique primitive experience close to home. Although it was partially logged and mined in the early 1900s, the mountain has retained its wild feel due to its steep slopes, lush flora, and unmaintained trail system. The top square mile

Cyclist foraging on Squak Mountain

of Squak, Section 4, was donated to Washington as a wilderness park in 1972. Although this designation excludes mountain bicycles, there are many trails on Squak that avoid Section 4. Unfortunately, the city of Issaquah has adopted a plan that, if enacted, would exclude mountain bicycles from the entire mountain; King County is working on a master plan that may eliminate bicycles from the mountain, including Section 9. In fact, some "No Bikes" signs may already be in place, even though regulations concerning bicycles do not yet exist. Call King County Open Space and the city of Issaquah to let them know you enjoy riding on Squak Mountain outside of Section 4 and that you would like to ride on Section 9.

To get there

Take Interstate 90 east to Exit 17 in Issaquah. Turn south onto Front Street. Begin from Issaquah's old train station, located just off the northeast corner of Front Street and Sunset Way in Issaquah. Park in the lot next to the old Great Northern steam engine.

The ride

Beginning from the old train station, ride to the intersection of Front Street and Sunset Way. Turn right and pedal west down Sunset Way. Reach the intersection of Sunset Way and Newport Way. Pass straight through this intersection and immediately begin climbing. The road, which becomes Mountain Park Blvd., climbs at a brutal rate. At **1.2 miles**, take a left fork onto Mountainside Drive S.W. and continue climbing.

At a hairpin, **1.6 miles**, find a gravel pullout. A trail exits from the back of the small parking area. Leave the pavement at this point and pedal up the wide, rocky, steep trail. There has been some logging here recently so walking may be necessary due to the sloppy, bulldozed road. At **2 miles**, reach a fork: take the left fork. A few pedal strokes farther, the trail forks again; this time take the right fork onto a narrow trail. (Do not take the left fork here because it quickly enters the wilderness park.) Just after a short, steep hill, **2.3 miles**, the trail arrives at a T. Take the right fork.

From the T, the trail begins dropping as it traverses the northwest flank of Squak Mountain. At **2.6 miles**, bypass a trail that cuts up the bank to the left. Continue down; there are several treacherous spots during the descent. At **3 miles**, reach a gate above State Rte. 900. At **3.2 miles**, turn right onto State Rte. 900. At **3.6 miles**, turn right onto a dirt road at an old yellow gate. **Whoa**, this is easy to miss. Just up the short hill, **3.7 miles**, reach an intersection. Take the left fork. The trail narrows and follows the power lines. At **3.75 miles**, when the trail hits a road, bear right and continue under the power lines. At **4.6 miles**, there is a series of trails—use your best instinct to stay on the main trail under the power lines. Just before the power lines start up a steep hill, the trail bends to the left into the woods. Stay on the main trail. At **5 miles**, turn right up a hill. At **5.2 miles**, find a single track on the right which leads to a paved road—12th Ave. N.W.

Turn right onto pavement, cycling up the hill. The road becomes Mount Olympus Dr. S.W. At **5.7 miles**, reach a T and turn left. This road becomes Sunset Way. Follow Sunset Way to the intersection of W. Sunset Way and Newport Way, **6.3 miles**. From here, take Sunset Way back to the old train station, **6.5 miles**.

Addition up Squak

From the T at 2.3 miles, turn left instead of right. The trail widens; after struggling up the trail for **.25 mile**, find a faint trail on the right just as the road hairpins to the left. Take this trail as it disappears into the woods. At **.4 mile**, the trail takes a sudden right and drops sharply. The trail turns left, levels, and crosses a creek. After crossing the creek, you'll have to walk up the opposite bank. At **.5 mile**, the unmaintained trail levels, traversing gradually upward. Pass by a faint trail on the right. At **.8 mile**, the trail becomes steep again. At **1.25 miles**, the trail tops out. A simple building is situated up a short road on the left. Riding out and back on this addition adds **2.5 miles** to the ride.

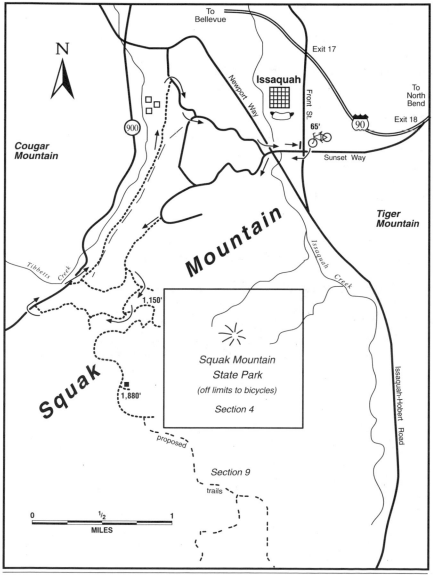

Ride 25 ✿ ✿✿✿ ✿

PRESTON RAILROAD TRAIL

Checklist: 11.6 miles, Loop; dirt trails, dirt roads
Duration: 2–4 hours
Hill factor: steep 3-mile climb to start, other short steep hills
Skill level: advanced
Season: summer, fall
Maps: USGS Hobart, Tiger Mountain State Forest map
Ownership: public
User density: medium; hikers, bicyclists
Hazards: jarring washboards on trail

Prelude

Although the first three miles climb steeply up a nondescript dirt road on East Tiger Mountain's south flank, some of the views are worth the sweat. The Preston Railroad Trail was a logging railroad grade early in this century. Recently the trail was scouted, built, and is now maintained by members of the Backcountry Bicycle Trails Club. The trail offers some excellent, winding sections, as well as a few jarring ones.

To get there

Drive east on Interstate 90 to Exit 25, the Highway 18 Exit. Drive south on Highway 18 for 4.5 miles. Find the parking area on the right just beyond the summit.

Tiger Mountain trailhead

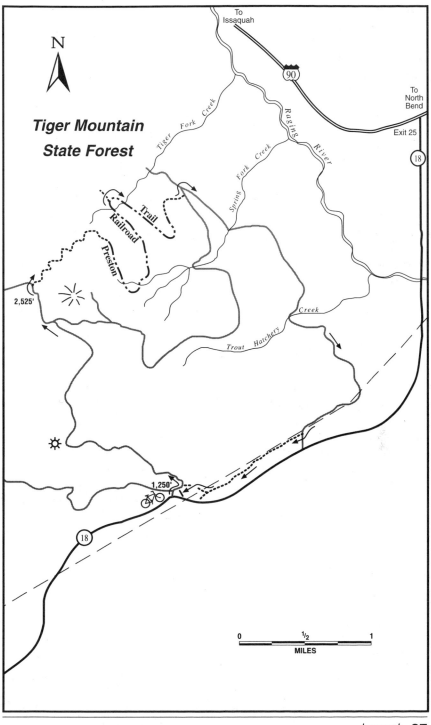

Tiger Mountain
State Forest

The ride

Two dirt roads exit from the north end of the parking lot. Take the right road, which is gated. Immediately the grade becomes steep, winding up the south side of East Tiger Mountain. Pass the Falls Trail (yet to be completed) on the right at **.3 miles**. As of autumn 1992, this trail is marked only by a ribbon. Continue up the road, a steep climb. Reach a viewpoint (a rest point!) at **1.4 miles**. From here you get great views of Mount Rainier as well as the Green, Cedar, and White River valleys. The worst of the climbing is now over. The grade continues to climb to a fork at **2.7 miles**. Take a left (the right fork goes to top, where you'll find the pleasant combination of picnic tables and microwave towers).

Whoa, at **3.1 miles** take a trail that exits the road off to the right. The long climb makes this turn easy to miss for anyone who has drifted deep into hallucinations due to lack of oxygen. Enter a deep forest, winding along a fun, twisting trail that demands some technical riding skill. The trail drops and then climbs a bit until it meets the old Preston railroad grade at **3.8 miles**. The railroad grade, straight and evenly sloped compared to the trail before, switchbacks around Tiger Mountain to the right, then descends, bumpy and jarring at times. Blowdown and wet trails make some walking inevitable on this section.

At **6.7 miles**, reach a road: take a left, downhill (right takes you to the top of Tiger). Ride a short distance to another road at **6.9 miles**. This time turn right and continue down. At **8.6 miles**, the road bottoms out and heads up. At **9.6 miles**, the road meets some power lines. Ride along the road beside the power lines, continuing clockwise around Tiger Mountain. **Whoa**, at **10.1 miles**, turn right, climbing steeply underneath the power lines, away from what appears to be the main road. (If you reach Highway 18, you have gone one-quarter mile too far.)

At **10.4 miles**, the road looks as though it goes up a steep, wide hill to the base of one of the power-line towers. Instead, take the trail that cuts around and below the tower on the left. The trail continues under the power lines, dropping then climbing as you go. Most riders will have to walk a short section near **11 miles**. At **11.3 miles**, take the lesser trail to the right that crosses under the power lines and goes into the woods (if you reach Highway 18, you have gone too far). Ride through the woods for less than one-quarter mile, then pop out onto the dirt road above the parking lot. Turn left, and drop down the road to the parking lot for a total **11.6 miles**.

Ride 26 ❁❁❁

FAT HAND TRAIL

Checklist: 4.2 miles, Loop; dirt trails, dirt roads
Duration: 1–2 hours
Hill factor: very steep trail up, some walking
Skill level: advanced
Season: late spring, summer, fall
Map: USGS Hobart, Tiger Mountain State Forest map
Ownership: public
User density: medium; hikers, bicyclists
Hazards: strenuous climb, cars

Prelude

Although this is a short ride, the trail is quite technical, and the climb is hectic. The route winds up through the forests of Tiger Mountain's south side. Strong riders could do this ride in tandem with the Preston Railroad Trail (page 96).

Gliding down an easy section of the Fat Hand Trail

To get there

Drive east on Interstate 90 to Exit 25, the Highway 18 Exit. Drive south on Highway 18 for 4.5 miles. Find the parking area on the right just beyond the summit.

The ride

Two dirt roads exit from the north end of the parking lot. Take the left road, the road with no gate. Ride out the dirt road. At **.4 mile**, find the Fat Hand Trail on the right side of the road. The trail immediately begins climbing. The trail forks at **.7 mile**: take the left fork, which crosses the creek. At **.9 mile**, arrive at a T: take the left trail, which winds around to a creek crossing.

The trail, which continues to climb, challenges even the experienced rider. Everyone should expect to walk part of this climb. Bypass a trail off to the right at **1.1 miles**. Ignore spur trails off to the right—stay on the main trail. At **1.5 miles**, cross another creek. The trail levels somewhat, then at **1.9 miles** it traverses a steep slope. At **2.6 miles**, the trail reaches a dirt road (West Side Road): turn left. Ride down West Side Road to the parking area, **4.2 miles**.

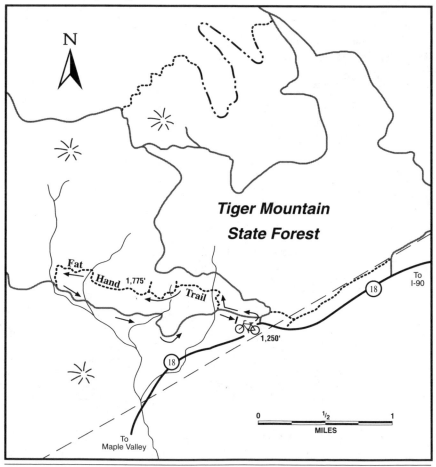

Ride 27 ✸✸

ISSAQUAH TO TIGER MOUNTAIN

Checklist: 7.4 miles, Loop; paved roads, dirt roads and trails
Duration: 1–3 hours
Hill factor: easy except for the steep climb from 1 to 2 miles, some walking
Skill level: intermediate
Season: spring, summer, fall
Maps: USGS Bellevue South, Tiger Mountain State Forest map
Ownership: City of Issaquah, Washington State Forests
User density: high; hikers, runners, bicyclists
Hazards: crossing under I-5 bridge, cars on Sunset Way

Prelude

This is a short, relatively easy ride across varied terrain—forested, suburban, urban—perfect for the strong, beginning rider. Since it begins in downtown Issaquah, you don't need to drive to the High Point Exit on Interstate 90 to experience the beauty of Tiger Mountain. Most of the trails on Tiger Mountain are closed to bicycles. Sometimes the Old Bus Trail is seasonally closed, and the State Department of Natural Resources (DNR) is considering banning mountain bicyclists altogther. If you enjoy the beauty of Tiger Mountain and want to continue to ride these trails, be courteous to other users and contact the DNR.

To get there

Take Interstate 90 east to Exit 17 in Issaquah. Turn south onto Front Street. Drive to Issaquah's old train station, located off the northeast corner of Front Street and Sunset Way. Park in the lot next to the old Great Northern steam donkey engine.

The ride

From the parking lot, pedal southeast along the railroad tracks. The steel rails extend only a short way past the station, but the railroad grade, which is dirt and gravel, continues straight, crossing several streets. At **.45 mile**, the railroad grade narrows. There are several neighborhood trails that spur off; stay on the main trail. At **.95 mile**, the railroad grade bends to the left and crosses Front Street S. Continue straight across the road to the trail on the opposite side. Just beyond this crossing, the trail meets some power lines, **1.2 miles**.

Pass a trail on the right, then at **1.25 miles**, reach an intersection and turn right and then immediately right again, following the sign for the Talus Caves. The dirt road climbs to a metal gate at **1.35 miles**; a sign explains that bicycles are allowed on posted trails only. At **1.85 miles**, after a serious climb up a dirt road through a lightly wooded area, ignore the trail off to the right; continue up the road. For the next one-quarter mile, there are several trails that spur off from the main trail. Continue straight up the main

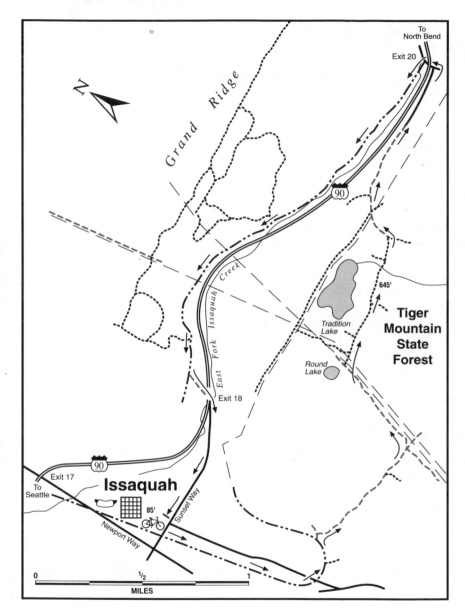

trail until, at a short hill, it pops out of the forested area. Bear up to the left, following the power lines. At **2.1 miles**, reach top of hill at of one of the power-line towers.

At **2.4 miles**, after the third power-line tower, take the Bus Road Trail on the right, which passes under the power lines. At **2.7 miles**, pass the hiker-only trail on the left to Tradition Lake. Continue straight. At **2.75 miles**, find the Old Bus. Stay on the main trail as it passes by numerous hiker-only trails. At **3.1 miles**, the main trail bears around to the left; ignore the hiker-only trail up to the right. At an intersection, **3.25 miles**,

Issaquah's Great Northern steam donkey engine

reach the power lines again; take the center route that crosses under the power lines.

At **3.65 miles**, reach the gate at the parking lot next to I-90. Ride along the road as if you were getting on I-90, turn left onto 270th S.E. and ride under the interstate, past the westbound entrance, then turn left into the first gravel parking area, **4.2 miles**. (See Grand Ridge, page 82.) Walk across the old bridge, then head down the railroad grade. Stay on the main road, passing several trails on the right. Take the first road that splits off left, down toward I-90, at **6.4 miles**. At **6.6 miles**, after a steep descent, the road seems to dead-end at the I-90. Find a small footbridge that crosses the creek and leads under I-90. On the opposite side of I-90, find a road, E. Sunset Way, and aim downhill to the right, **6.7 miles**. From here, ride into Issaquah to the intersection of Sunset Way and Front Street, **7.3 miles**, and find the old Train Station on the right.

Ride 28 ☻☻

LAKE SAWYER

Checklist: 5.7 miles, Loop; paved roads, dirt roads and trails
Duration: 1–2 hours
Hill factor: flat with a couple slight rollers
Skill level: intermediate
Season: all year
Map: USGS Auburn
Ownership: private
User density: low; hikers, equestrians, motorbikers, bicyclists
Hazards: cars, motorcycles, real estate development

Prelude

There always needs to be a reason to go the bakery in Black Diamond. Herein lies the purpose of this ride. Beginning in Black Diamond, the route crosses country highways, lightly forested single track, and wide gravel roads. Advanced riders probably want to ride more than one loop and may wish to explore other trails. Unfortunately, real estate development has already bulldozed some of the best trails in this area.

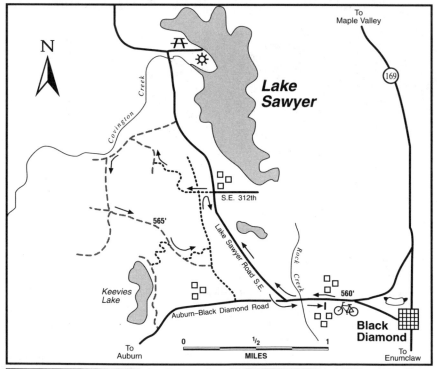

To get there

Take Interstate 405 south to Exit 4 near Renton. Take Highway 169 south to Black Diamond. Just before entering Black Diamond, turn right onto Roberts Road. Drive .9 mile to the King County Library on the left. Park in the library's lot.

The ride

Beginning from the King County Library parking lot, turn left onto Roberts Road (Auburn–Black Diamond Road). Pedal **.5 mile** and turn right onto Lake Sawyer Road S.E. Ride to S.E. 312th Street, **1.5 miles**, and turn left, off the pavement and onto a dirt trail. After about 50 yards, reach a four-way intersection. Find the trail straight across the intersection and continue. The trail immediately narrows, winding through the trees. This is the only technical section of this ride.

When the trail reaches a gravel road at **1.9 miles**, bear left. At **2.2 miles**, the road forks: take the main road to the right. Arrive at a T at **2.3 miles** and turn left. At **2.6 miles**, the road divides: stay on the main road to the left. Reach a four-way intersection at **2.9 miles** and bear left. The gravel road narrows somewhat and descends. Bypass a trail on the right at **3.3 miles**.

At **3.5 miles**, find a narrow dirt trail on the left and take it. When the single track reaches a T at **3.8 miles**, turn left. At **4.1 miles**, arrive at the four-way intersection that you passed through early in the ride—turn right and retrace your steps. Quickly, meet Lake Sawyer Road S.E. and turn right. Turn left upon reaching the Auburn–Black Diamond Road at **5.2 miles**. Return to the King County Library at **5.7 miles** to complete the loop.

Looking down the trail near Lake Sawyer

Ride 29 🏵🏵🏵

LAKE DESIRE

Checklist: 9.6 miles, Loop; dirt trails, dirt roads, paved roads
Duration: 1–3 hours
Hill factor: several difficult hills
Skill level: advanced
Season: summer
Map: USGS Renton
Ownership: public and private
User density: medium; equestrians, bicyclists, hikers
Hazards: magnetic emissions from power lines, mud puddles

Prelude

Lake Desire is a wild and crazy ride through mud bogs, under power lines, along paved roads, and through lots of water. The dry months of summer are the best time for this ride, otherwise you'll be slopping through buckets of mud and you are guaranteed to pedal into a puddle that's deeper than your hubs.

To get there

Go south on Interstate 405 to Exit 4. Take Highway 169, the Maple Valley Road, heading south. Turn right onto 140th Way S.E. Proceed 2 miles, then turn left on Petrovitsky Road. Drive 1.4 miles farther, then turn right onto Old Petrovitsky Road. Drive .6 mile farther and find the unnamed King County Park on the right. Park in the gravel lot.

The ride

Start from the gravel parking area at the King County Park. Pedaling, continue east on Old Petrovitsky Road. At **.1 mile**, Old Petrovitsky Road intersects with Petrovitsky Road. Go straight, crossing Petrovitsky Road, onto S.E. 184th. At **.5 mile**, the road bends to the left and becomes W. Lake Desire Dr. S.E. Ride down the hill and then up. Just as the road rises and bends to the right, **.8 mile**, look up to the left and find a faint trail that follows a small set of power lines away from Lake Desire Dr. **Whoa**, this is an easy trail to miss.

Pedal along the trail (which becomes a jeep trail) to a four-way intersection at **1.3 miles**. Continue straight. Reach a muddy T at **1.5 miles**, and turn right. The jeep trail quickly divides again. Again take the right fork, which climbs a mound and becomes a narrow trail in the woods. **Whoa**, this turn is also quite easy to miss. (The left fork will cut one-quarter mile of mud trail off the ride.) Immediately, **1.6 miles**, the trail forks: turn right. Slog through the mud for a short distance, then at **1.9 miles**, find a fork in the trail and turn left.

At the **2.1-mile mark**, reach a water tower and bear around to the left until you

Exploring the miles of wild and crazy trails near Lake Desire

meet a road. At the road, turn right and pedal to the set of three huge power lines. About 50 yards farther, turn right onto a road that runs under the near edge of the power lines. The road drops and then climbs. At the top of the hill, **2.6 miles** and still under the power lines, jog left to a road under the center of the power lines. Continue following the power lines. The road descends again, and at **3.2 miles**, runs between barbed-wire fences. Just after the fence on the right ends, find a trail on the right, **3.5 miles**. Follow this trail to a paved road, **3.6 miles**.

Pedal down the road to the **3.7-mile mark**, and turn left onto S.E. 168th Street. At **3.9 miles**, turn right onto 188th Ave. S.E. Reach a T at **4 miles**: turn left onto S.E. 170th Street. Less than 100 yards farther, take the dirt trail on the right that exits the paved street between some large rocks. At **4.2 miles**, the trail divides—turn right. This next section is often very wet. Wood rounds have been placed across the trail to help keep it dry. But these can be treacherous when wet. At **4.4 miles**, bypass a trail on the left. At **4.7 miles**, the trail veers to the left and begins climbing. The trail climbs steadily. Ignore lesser trails during the climb. At **5.2 miles**, take the left fork.

At **5.6 miles**, the trail meets a gravel road: turn left, downhill. Bypass a trail on the right. Ride down the road to a four-way intersection between the road and a trail at **5.7 miles**. Turn right onto the trail. The trail forks at **5.9 miles**: take the left fork. At **6.3 miles**, pedal straight through a four-way intersection. Just up the trail, bypass a spur on the right: stay on the main trail. The trail reaches a T at **6.6 miles**: turn right. Ignore the left-hand trail at **6.8 miles**. When the trail forks again at **7 miles**, turn left and quickly reach a dirt road. Pedal down the road, and meet Petrovitsky Road at **7.3 miles**.

From Petrovitsky Road, turn right and ride to the first intersection. Cross Petrovitsky Road, and find a trail alongside a fence that parallels the road. Take the trail to the right (left goes around Lake Youngs, see page 109). Ride the trail that follows the fence to a fork at **9.4 miles**. Turn right, leaving the fence. At **9.6 miles**, reach the gravel parking area, completing the loop.

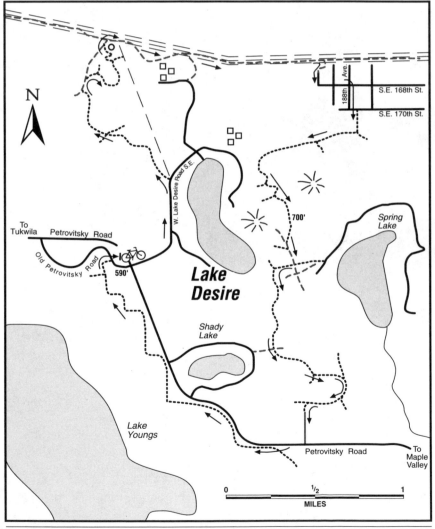

Ride 30 ❀❀

LAKE YOUNGS

Checklist: 9.9 miles, Loop; dirt trails, dirt roads
Duration: 1–2 hours
Hill factor: one difficult hill, mostly easy rolling hills
Skill level: beginner, with some rough sections
Season: all year
Map: USGS Renton
Ownership: public
User density: medium to high; equestrians, bicyclists, hikers
Hazards: horse pucky, rough trail in places

Prelude

Lake Youngs is part of the Seattle water system. Because of this, the lake is surrounded by a tall fence, and the security is tight. The lake is never actually visible, but ignore that frustration and enjoy this easy, wooded loop.

Photo by Greg Strong

Pedaling the Lake Youngs path

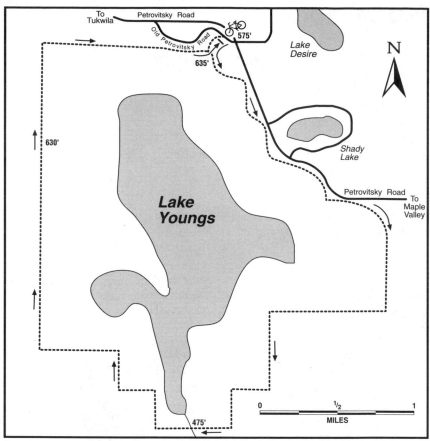

To get there

Go south on Interstate 405 to Exit 4. Take Highway 169 heading south. Turn right onto 140th Way S.E. Proceed 2 miles, then turn left on Petrovitsky Road. Drive 1.4 miles farther, then turn right onto Old Petrovitsky Road. Drive .6 mile further and find the unnamed King Country Park on the right. Park in the gravel lot.

The ride

Begin from the gravel parking area at the King County Park next to Lake Youngs. Find the trail that leaves from the parking area. This trail accesses the loop around Lake Youngs. At **.15 mile** from the parking area, reach the Lake Youngs loop trail and turn left. The jeep trail follows the fence that encloses the resevoir. At **2.3 miles**, reach the intersection of 184th S.E. and S.E. Lake Youngs Road. Cross over the water pipe and continue following the jeep trail alongside the fence. At **6.5 miles**, reach the corner of 148th Ave. S.E. and S.E. 216th Street. Take a right, following the fence and paralleling 148th S.E. At **9.6 miles**, reach the bottom of a short, but steep, hill. You may have to walk it. At **9.75 miles**, you've completed the loop. Take a left onto the trail that returns to the parking area, **9.9 miles**.

Ride 31 ✪

LAKE WILDERNESS

Checklist: 3 miles, Out & Back; dirt and gravel trails
Duration: 1 hour
Hill factor: flat
Skill level: beginner
Season: all year
Maps: USGS Auburn, USGS Renton
Ownership: public
User density: medium; equestrians, some bikers, walkers
Hazards: deep, loose gravel

Prelude

This is an easy, flat ride that traverses an old railroad grade above Lake Wilderness. The grade passes through light forests and by a new housing development, all with views of the lake below. It's perfect for a beginner mountain bicyclist because there is an extra four miles of riding if you're feeling motivated.

To get there

Take Interstate 405 to Exit 4. Catch Highway 169, the Maple Valley Road, southeast toward Maple Valley. Drive several miles past Maple Valley, then turn right onto Witte Road S.E. Travel .8 mile, and turn left onto S.E. 248th Street. After less than one-half mile, find Lake Wilderness Park on the left. Park in the lot.

Herons on Lake Wilderness

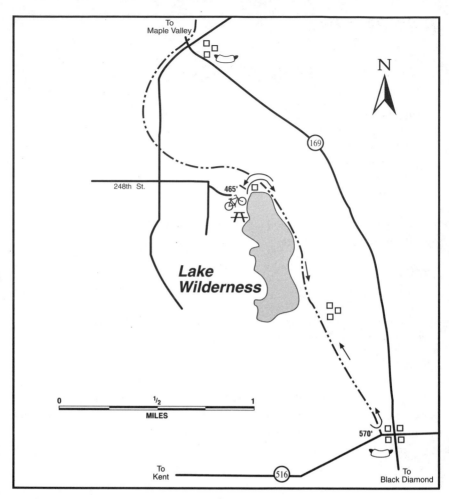

The ride

Beginning from the parking lot of Lake Wilderness Park, ride toward the park buildings at the north end of the lake. Pass through a gate and find a wide dirt path that bears to the right, behind the buildings. Stay on the main path toward a short, steep hill. Walk up the hill and find the gravel railroad grade, **.2 mile**. Turn right, riding to a gate. Pass through the gate and continue along the gravel trail. The trail traverses the east side of Lake Wilderness. Stay on the main trail, riding past some new homes, until you reach Highway 516, the Kent-Kangley Road, at **1.7 miles**. Turn around here and retrace your steps. The return trip makes the ride **3.4 miles** long.

Addition

If you still want more when you get back to the gate, continue north on the railroad grade. It winds about two more miles until it ends at Highway 169. Turn around here and retrace your steps. This adds about four miles onto the ride.

Ride 32 ✿ ✿✿✿ ✿

SKOOKUM FLATS TRAIL

Checklist: 11.5 miles, Loop; trails, dirt roads
Duration: 2–4 hours
Hill factor: rolling hills, some steep sections with short walks
Skill level: expert
Season: summer, early fall
Maps: Green Trails Greenwater, USGS Suntop, USGS White River Park
Ownership: public
User density: extremely high; hikers, bicyclists
Hazards: technical riding, slippery bridges and roots when wet

Prelude

True, this is a little over an hour's drive from Seattle, but it's such an enjoyable ride it can't be excluded on a technicality. One author called this Washington's best ride. Although I wouldn't bestow that honor on the Skookum Trail, it is a most excellent ride: extremely technical, through old growth, along the rugged White River. But since this trail is so heavily used, it's best to avoid it on weekends.

To get there

From Enumclaw, drive east on Highway 410 just over 28 miles to Camp Sheppard on the left. Continuing east on Highway 410 for about 1.5 miles, find a bridge on the right that spans the White River at Buck Creek. Park at a small parking space next to Highway 410.

Photo by Peter Zilly

Crossing a bridge on the Skookum Flats trail

The ride

From the intersection of the Buck Creek Road and Highway 410, ride down the Buck Creek Road, immediately crossing the White River. Just after the bridge, find the Skookum Flats Trail, #1194, on the right, **.1 mile**. At **.3 mile**, take the right fork. The trail, which traverses a precipitous slope, has many roots and tight turns. At **1.3 miles**, reach a rocky, uphill section that must be walked. At **1.4 miles**, reach the White River Footbridge, an old suspension bridge that leads to Highway 410. Just before the bridge, turn left and find the trail that veers away from the river, climbing for the next .25 mile up steps, roots, and large rocks. The trail levels out at **1.6 miles**. At **1.75 miles**, take

A Douglas fir along the White River

the right fork, traversing the bank above the White River. Some walking will be necessary through this section.

The trail becomes less difficult, and at **4.8 miles** reach a clearing and a camp site. From the camp, take the right fork, staying along the river. At **5 miles**, the road forks. Again, go right, following the jeep trail. At **5.2 miles**, the trail becomes single track, winding through some gigantic Douglas firs. Stay on the main trail. At **5.8 miles**, reach the paved road. Turn right onto the paved road. After crossing the bridge, **5.9 miles**, find a trail, #1204A, on the right that brings you to the Dalles Campground. At **6.4 miles**, just before entering the Dalles Campground, you'll find a Douglas fir that is 9.6 feet in diameter; it is estimated to be around 700 years old.

From the huge tree, ride through the campground to the entrance of Dalles Campground, **6.9 miles**. Cross Highway 410 and ride up the dirt road, #7150. At **7.1 miles**, the road levels and bends to the right, then bends left and parallels the highway. Stay on the main road: there are many driveways to cabins along this way. At **8 miles**, reach Highway 410 again. Turn left onto it. At **8.6 miles**, find a small, unmarked trail on the left side of the road. **Whoa**, this is a difficult trail to find. It looks like it could be a one-car turnoff on the left side. The trail climbs up a short bank away from Highway 410, then meets some power lines and bears to the right. After a steep, but short, climb, the trail divides at the top, **8.75 miles**. Turn left here, away from the power lines, onto the White River Trail, #1199. Ride through the woods, climbing to the **8.9-mile point**, where you'll find another trail junction. Stay on the White River Trail. Reach another intersection at **9.2 miles**; again continue straight on #1199.

At **9.65 miles**, enter a clearing that denotes the edge of Camp Sheppard. At **9.7 miles**, the trail comes out to a road. Then at **9.75 miles**, with some buildings on the right, find a trail and trail sign off to left. **Whoa**, this is hard to find. Find the trail and turn right, riding above the buildings at Camp Sheppard. After this turn, stay on the main trail. At **10 miles**, arrive at another intersection: continue straight on #1199. At **10.3 miles**, reach another intersection: again continue straight on #1199. At **11.4 miles**, arrive at yet another intersection; this time turn right, leaving the White River Trail. Ride about thirty yards down to Highway 410. Cross it, turn left, and ride up the highway. At **11.5 miles**, return to the small parking area.

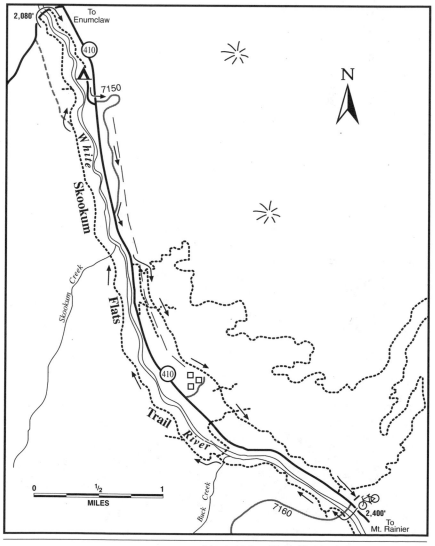

Ride 33 ✹ ✹ ✹ ✹ ✹

NOBLE KNOB

Checklist: 22.2 miles, Loop; dirt trails, dirt roads
Duration: 4–7 hours
Hill factor: huge elevation gains, steep up and down, many dismounts
Skill level: expert
Season: summer, early fall
Maps: Green Trails Greenwater, Green Trails Lester
Ownership: public
User density: high; hikers, bicyclists
Hazards: technical riding, trail along cliffs

Prelude

Tough, rugged, and dangerous, this is an incredibly beautiful ride through a thick Douglas fir and pine forest. With Mount Rainier acting as a beacon to the west and the spectacular, precipitous palisades dropping away from the trail's edge into the White River Valley, this loop is both intense and wild. The White River Ranger District has done a great job to keep this trail open to bicyclists.

To get there

Take Interstate 405 to Exit 4. Catch Highway 169, the Maple Valley Road, south to Enumclaw. From Enumclaw, drive east (and south) on Highway 410 toward Mount Rainier for about 31 miles. Just past mile post 56, find a dirt road, #7174, on the left. Drive 6.6 miles up this road to Corral Pass. Park in the small dirt lot on the left.

Mount Rainier from Dalles Ridge

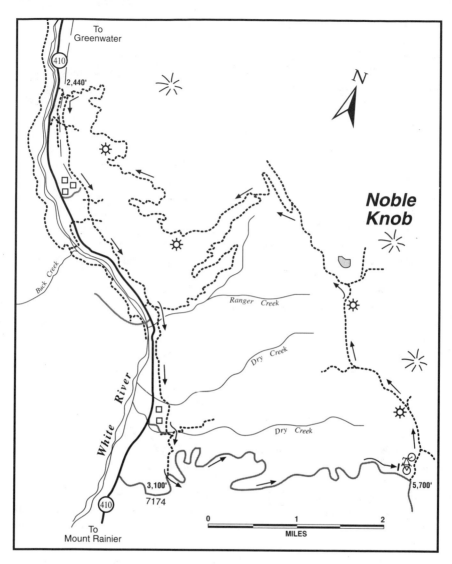

To Greenwater

410

2,440'

Noble Knob

N

Buck Creek

Ranger Creek

Dry Creek

White River

Dry Creek

3,100'
7174

410

To Mount Rainier

5,700'

| 0 | | 1 | | 2 |

MILES

The ride

Starting at Corral Pass, find the Noble Knob Trail, #1184. Ride just over **.5 mile** to a T at a primitive road and turn left, down the road. The road becomes a trail, levels, and traverses north, following the contours. This section of trail is lightly forested, and Mount Rainier is in your face to the left. Stay on the main double track, ignoring the lesser spurs. Reach a fork at **1.5 miles**. Take the trail that begins on the left.

After a short climb to the top of a ridge that provides huge views of the Norse Peak Wilderness, Mount Rainier, Mount Adams, and beyond, drop down to an intersection at **1.9 miles**. Stay right on Noble Knob Trail, #1184, toward 28 Mile Road. Continue through the woods, traversing the side of Dalles Ridge. After several short, steep switchbacks (walk, if necessary, to preserve the trail), reach an intersection at **3 miles**. See Noble Knob (an oxymoron?) across the ridge. The Noble Knob Trail divides right and enters the Norse Peak Wilderness. Instead, turn left onto the Dalles Ridge Trail, #1173. A small lake sits in a pocket below this intersection; in the distance the Olympics and Mount Baker are visible beyond the clearcuts.

The trail continues traversing the ridge, in and out of the trees, providing incredible views of Mount Rainier. At **4.2 miles** the trail divides: take the left fork down the Ranger Creek Trail, #1197. The trail drops quickly for the next mile, and at **5.3 miles**, it reaches a camping shelter and a fork in the trail. (The left fork drops down Ranger Creek Trail and meets Buck Creek Trail after 4.8 miles—a safer and shorter route.) Instead, go around the shelter to find the right fork, the Palisades Trail, #1198. (Depending on logging schedules, you may be forced to take the Ranger Creek Trail.)

From the shelter, ride along the less-maintained trail that traverses the ridge above Little Ranger Peak. At **6.5 miles**, reach an amazing viewpoint, looking out from the top of the Palisades. Over the next three miles, the trail winds generally downhill through the woods, often finding the edge of these cliffs that overlook the White River Valley. The trail is rough, and riding along the edge of the Palisades is dangerous for cyclists who suffer from vertigo. At **8.0 miles**, cross a bridge over a small creek.

From here the trail drops more steadily, but ascends to the edge of the cliffs at **9.6 miles**. Shortly, the trail begins a series of switchbacks that become progressively steeper and more severe. Around **10.3 miles**, the trail becomes too steep to ride. Hoist your bike onto your shoulder and scramble down the switchbacks for about one-half mile.

At **11.6 miles**, reach an intersection: turn left onto the White River Trail, #1199. Stay on White River Trail, bypassing a junction at **11.9 miles**. At **12.4 miles**, reach a clearing that marks the edge of Camp Sheppard. Then at **12.5 miles**, with some buildings on the right, find a trail and trail sign on the left. **Whoa**, this is hard to find. Find the trail and turn right, riding above the buildings at Camp Sheppard. After this turn, stay on the main trail, bypassing several spurs. At **12.75 miles**, arrive at another intersection: continue straight on #1199. At **13 miles**, reach another intersection: again continue straight on #1199.

The trail gradually climbs. At **14.1 miles**, ignore a short spur down to the right to Highway 410—continue straight. Just up the hill, reach a fork: the Ranger Creek Trail cuts up to the left. Instead, continue straight on White River Trail toward Corral Pass Road. At **15.6 miles**, the trail divides upon arriving at Deep Creek. Take the left fork upstream. At **15.8 miles**, after a dismount, take the right fork and cross the bridge.

Reach Corral Pass Road at **16.3 miles**. From here, turn left and ride up to the top of Corral Pass to complete the ride, **22.2 miles**. The last five miles are grueling, gaining 2,700 feet and battling all sorts of motorized vehicles. Less ambitious riders may want to leave a second car near the bottom of the Corral Pass Road.

Ride 34 ❈ ❈ ❈ ❈

CAPITOL FOREST—PORTER CREEK

Checklist: 21.5 miles, Loop; dirt trails, some dirt roads
Duration: 3–7 hours
Hill factor: steady uphill first 7 miles, then easy up and down
Skill level: intermediate
Season: spring, summer, fall
Map: Washington State Dept. of Natural Resources: Capitol Forest
Ownership: Washington State Department of Natural Resources
User density: medium; equestrians, hikers, bicyclists
Hazards: mud, fatigue, getting lost

Prelude

Capitol Forest contains some of the best mountain biking in Western Washington: miles and miles of dirt trails for all skill levels through a beautiful forest. Currently, published mountain-bicycle trails send cyclists to the north side of the forest, the motorized side. But bicycles are legal on the nonmotorized, south side trails as well. These trails are rough and subsequently more technical than trails on the north side.

To get there

Take Interstate 5 south to Exit 88. Take Highway 12 west toward Rochester and Oakville. Continue on Highway 12 to the hamlet of Porter, an easy town to miss. From Porter, drive up Porter Creek Road, following the signs to the Porter Creek Campground. At 3.5 miles, reach an intersection: here the road becomes the B-Line. Follow the signs toward Porter Creek Camp about 1 mile further. Park at the campground.

The ride

From the campground, continue up B-Line Road. At **.3 mile**, the road forks: take the right fork, B-1000. At **.6 mile**, the Green Line Trail #6 exits the road on the left. Take the trail, riding to the **.8-mile point** where the trail divides: take the right fork toward Wedekind Camp and immediately cross the North Fork of Porter Creek, wading. Just after the creek the trail meets road B-1000 again: take a left. At **1 mile**, when the road forks, take the lesser right fork that stays low, next to the creek. At **1.6 miles**, the road ends, but just before the end take a trail on the left, which traverses through mud and rocks to a bridge, **1.75 miles**.

After the bridge the trail divides: take the left fork which climbs up the Iron Creek drainage. For the next three-quarters of a mile, climb up the small alder-soaked valley, through more mud and rocks and up several switchbacks. At **2.5 miles**, the trail, still steadily up, turns to a pine-needle carpet, and the riding becomes much easier. At **3.7 miles**, the trail levels somewhat and traverses to the **3.9-mile mark** where, after crossing a bridge, the trail continues the steep climb toward Camp Wedekind.

An old railroad grade in Capitol Forest

The trail, rough and technical in places, meets an old dirt road, at **4.8 miles**. Turn right, pedal about 100 yards along the road, then take the trail on the left. If you continue up the road, you'll get to the same place, but why not ride trail? At **6.6 miles**, reach an intersection. Take Trail #30 right, toward Wedekind Camp. At **7.1 miles**, the trail finally descends for a pitch then hits a road; continue down the road. At **7.2 miles**, hit another road and take a left. A few pedal strokes farther, reach an intersection at Camp Wedekind. Turn right and ride down the road to a faint trail on the left at **7.5 miles**, Trail #40. Turn up this trail which is an old railroad grade. At times the trail is overgrown and seems sketchy.

At **8.5 miles**, reach the intersection of Trail #40 and Trail #8. Turn right—away from the railroad grade—onto Mima-Porter Trail #8. The next six miles are less used and may not seem like the proper route. Follow the maps and use your best judgment. The trail drops, passing through some rough sections to a road, at **9.9 miles**. Stay down to the left. At **10.5 miles**, continue downhill on a double track. Right away, cross a dirt road and find the trail on the opposite side. After a fun downhill around **12.3 miles**, the trail parallels a road for a short distance—don't get on the road. Just past a bridge, **12.6 miles**, the trail dumps out onto a grass-covered road. Take a right onto the road. About 30 yards down the road, a trail exits to the right. Take the trail. Again at **13 miles**, the trail dumps out onto a road. Take a right, cross the road, and immediately take the trail off to the left. At **13.4 miles**, the trail reaches a main road—take a left on the road, then immediately take a right onto a trail. The trail parallels the road for a short distance, then crosses the road and continues on the opposite side. At **14 miles**, the trail bends close to a road on the left, but then veers away from it and climbs a hillside. At **14.8 miles**, pass by a swamp on the right. Just across a bridge the trail reaches a T—turn left.

At **16.1 miles**, after an easy climb out of a drainage, reach the intersection of roads C 1000 and C 1700. Turn right onto C 1000. At **16.6 miles**, arrive at the intersection of C-Line and C 1000: take a left down C-Line. At **18.3 miles**, pass a trail on the left; continue down the road. Take the C-Line all the way to Porter Creek Camp, passing lesser roads at **19.2 miles** (C 1800 on the left) and at **19.8 miles** (C 100 on the right). Continue down C-Line to the intersection of B-Line and C-Line, **20.6 miles**. This is the Porter entrance to the Capitol Forest. At the four-way intersection, bear to the right. At **21.5 miles**, arrive at the Porter Creek Campground and the car.

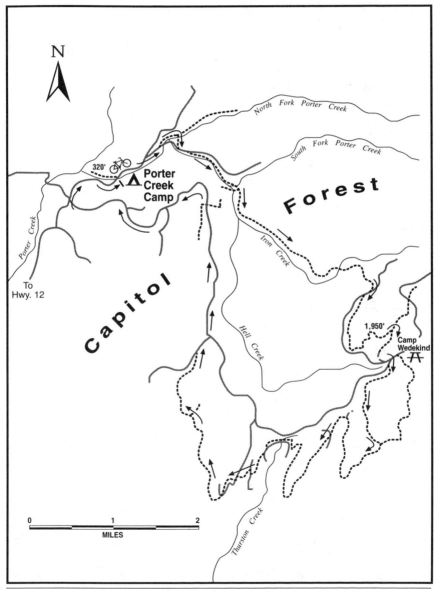

Ride 35 ✿✿✿✿

CAPITOL FOREST—MIMA CREEK

Checklist: 22.7 miles, Loop; dirt trails, some dirt roads
Duration: 3–7 hours
Hill factor: relentless up and down the entire way
Skill level: intermediate
Season: spring, summer, fall
Map: Washington State Dept. of Natural Resources: Capitol Forest
Ownership: Washington State Department of Natural Resources
User density: high; equestrians, hikers, bicyclists
Hazards: rough trails, fatigue, getting lost

Prelude

Just south of Puget Sound, Capitol Forest harbors miles of awesome mountain biking, much of it quite rigorous. The loose rocky trails and sharp hills on this ride demand stamina and riding skill. But the beautiful lush forest makes the hills more nuisances than lung-busters. Like the Porter Creek ride (page 119), Mima Creek is also located on the nonmotorized side of Capitol Forest. You won't be bothered by engines, although you need to be aware that equestrians and hikers use these trails extensively.

To get there

Take Interstate 5 south to Exit 95. Take Highway 121 west, past Littlerock to a T and turn right. Drive 2.5 miles, and just after entering Capitol Forest, find the Margaret McKenny Campground and trailhead on the left. Drive into the camp area (take note of the trailhead on the right immediately after the entrance) and park in the gravel lot.

The ride

From the campground parking area, ride back toward the entrance (200 yards) and find the Green Line #6 access trail. Stay on the main trail—ignoring spurs—as it winds down to Waddell Creek. Turn right and pedal for a short distance to a rickety suspension bridge, **.4 mile**. Cross the bridge and ride up the trail. The trail switchbacks up to a T: turn right (ignore the "DO NOT ENTER" trail on the left). Pedal to a road at **.6 mile**; turn right onto the road. Immediately take a trail off to the right. Stay on the main trail, bypassing several other trails. At **.9 mile**, reach a fork: stay on the main trail left toward the Mima Trailhead.

At **1.1 miles**, arrive at the Green Line #6, turn left toward the Mima Trailhead. At **1.6 miles**, the trail crosses a gravel road and continues on the other side. Just a few pedal strokes farther, reach another road: again find the rocky trail on the opposite side. When the trail divides at **2 miles**, turn right, continuing toward the Mima Trailhead. At **2.2 miles**, pass a trail on the left, continue on the main trail. At **2.8 miles**, reach the Mima Trailhead, and turn right onto the Mima-Porter Trail #8. Reach a fork at a wide portion

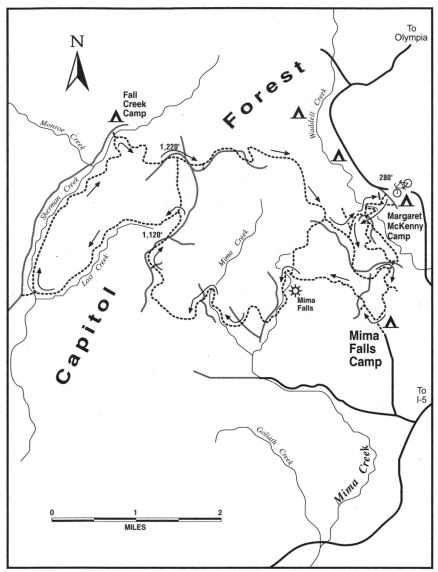

of the trail, **3.1 miles**, and veer right. After several more pedal strokes, cross a road. Continue on the trail toward Mima Falls. At **3.9 miles**, ride into a clearcut; stay on the main trail—ignore a series of faint spur trails. At **4.5 miles**, reach an intersection, turn left, staying on Mima-Porter Trail #8.

Arrive at Mima Falls, **4.9 miles**. The state has built a nice bench that overlooks the falls. Unfortunately, various travelers have left banana peels, cigarette butts, and plastic wrappers to spoil the view of the falls. At **5.5 miles**, after a downhill traverse to a bridge and short climb, reach a road. Continue on the trail across the road. The trail crosses another road at **5.9 miles**. Ride straight across another road at **7 miles**, to the trail on

the opposite side. A little farther, a long hill begins, and the trail climbs up to **8.1 miles** where it levels somewhat. Stay on the main trail; ignoring the short spur roads. At **8.5 miles**, ride across another road to the trail opposite. Excellent views on a clear day. At a four-way intersection, **9 miles**, continue straight on the main trail.

At **9.4 miles**, reach an intersection of gravel roads—D-4000 and D-5000. Find the trail diagonally across the intersection. At a fork in the trail, **9.9 miles**, turn left, staying on Mima-Porter Trail #8. (A right turn onto Trail #20 shortens the ride considerably.) From the intersection, the rocky trail descends along Lost Creek to its confluence with Sherman Creek at **12.3 miles**. Just

Tiptoeing across the suspension bridge near McKenny Campground

before Sherman Creek, the trail divides: turn right, riding up Sherman Creek on Mima-Porter Trail #8. The trail up Sherman Creek changes from smooth to muddy to rocky, crossing numerous bridges in various states of repair.

At **15.2 miles**, reach the junction with Green Line Trail #6. Turn right onto Trail #6, toward the McKenny Camp. (Fall Creek Camp sits across Sherman Creek to the left.) From here, the climbing begins in earnest. Cross a road to the trail on the other side, **17.2 miles**. Pass Trail #20 on the right at **17.4 miles**: stay on Trail #6, left. At **17.7 miles**, cross a road. At **17.9 miles**, ignore a trail off to the right; stay on the single track. At **18.2 miles**, the trail parallels a gravel road. Cross gravel roads at **18.7 miles** and **18.9 miles**. From here the trail drops quickly down a very rough trail. At **21.1 miles**, a gravel road marks the junction of Trail #6 and Trail #10. Turn left just before the road, staying on Green Line Trail #6 toward McKenny Camp. When the trail forks at **21.6 miles**, things should start looking familiar: you have completed the loop. Turn left onto Trail #6A. From this intersection, follow the signs to the rickety suspension bridge and the McKenny Camp parking area, **22.7 miles**.

Ride 36 ✵✵✵

DASH POINT

Checklist: 4.1 miles, Loop; dirt trails, paved road
Duration: 1–2 hours
Hill factor: rolling hills, required walking
Skill level: intermediate
Season: spring, summer, fall
Map: Dash Point State Park map
Ownership: public
User density: high; hikers, bicyclists
Hazards: stairs on trail

Prelude

Dash Point State Park is a busy campground during the summer, especially on weekends, so the riding is probably best during the week. The narrow, dirt trails through the wooded park near the campground provide fun, occasionally technical trail riding. Because of several steep slopes, stairs have been built to improve the trail. These must be walked. Be extremely courteous to all other trail users. The ranger has said that mountain bicycles are allowed "for the time being," meaning as long as there aren't too many complaints.

Puget Sound from the beach at Dash Point

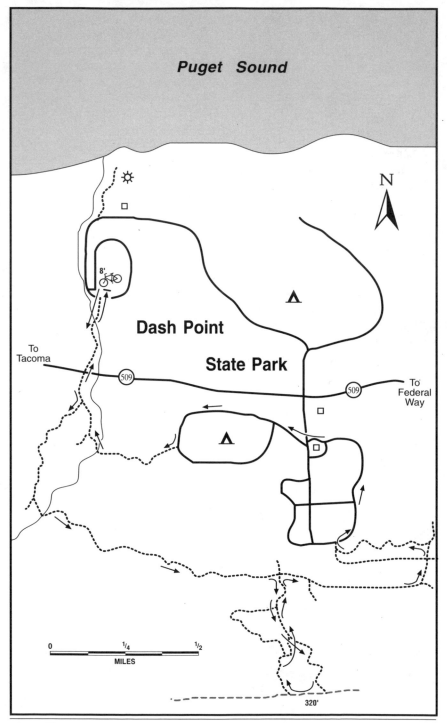

Puget Sound

N

Dash Point
State Park

To
Tacoma

509

509

To
Federal
Way

8'

0   1/4   1/2
MILES

320'

To get there

From Interstate 5, take Federal Way Exit 143 and travel west on S. 320th Street. Drive 4.6 miles until S.W. 320th Street ends. Turn right onto 47th Ave. S.W. Go less than one-half mile, and turn left onto S.W. Dash Point Road. Travel almost one mile to Dash Point State Park. Turn right into the day-use area; take the first left and drive down the hill to the parking lot near the beach.

The ride

From the parking lot near the beach, ride away from the beach. Find the trail that travels under the Highway 509 bridge far above. Pedal up the wide trail to **.3 mile** where you'll find a trail up the bank to the right. The walking begins. Push your bike about 250 yards up the trail before you can ride again. At **.4 mile**, cross a creek and continue up. The trail elbows left upon reaching the top of the hill at **.5 mile**. At **.8 mile**, walk across a bridge.

Reach a four-way intersection at **1 mile**. Turn up the hill to the right. The trail forks twice over the next quarter-mile: each time take the left trail. When the trail divides again at **1.4 miles**, turn right onto a wider jeep trail. Turn right, back onto a single-track trail, at **1.5 miles**. At **1.7 miles**, continue on the main trail—straight. At **1.75 miles**, take the left fork. This trail returns you to the earlier four-way intersection, **2 miles**. Turn right at the four-way intersection.

At **2.15 and 2.5 miles**, take the left fork each time. Just past the second fork, reach a four-way intersection: go straight. At **2.65 miles**, take the sharp, left fork. At **3 miles**, meet a wide trail and turn right. A few pedal strokes farther, reach campsite #58. Turn right onto the paved road. At **3.1 miles**, stay to the right, then at **3.3 miles** reach the park entrance.

From the pay station at the park entrance, turn right. Ride around the campsite loop counterclockwise, to campsite #15. Find the sign toward the beach. Turn right onto the trail toward the beach, **3.6 miles**. Walk down the wooden steps at **3.7 miles**. Then ride down the main trail—ignoring spurs—back to the parking lot, and the beach, at the beginning of the ride, **4.1 miles**.

Ride 37 ✿✿

BLAKE ISLAND

Checklist: 3.9 miles, Loop; wide dirt trails
Duration: 1–2 hour
Hill factor: rolling hills, several steep that require walking
Skill level: beginner
Season: all year
Map: USGS Duwamish Head, Blake Island State Park map
Ownership: public, short private section
User density: medium; hikers, bicyclists

Prelude

Some believe that Chief Seattle was born on Blake Island. In 1900 William Trimble bought the island and built a large estate which is now gone. Despite the history of past development, Blake Island seems wild and undisturbed, taking its cue from Chief Seattle. The perimeter trail around Blake Island, wide, hilly, and forested, provides some limited but wonderful views of Puget Sound.

To get there

The only way to get to Blake Island is by boat. You can either commandeer a friend who has a boat, or, from May through October, boats depart (about $20) from the Seattle waterfront toward Blake Island's barbecued salmon feasts at Tillicum Village. Bicycles are permitted on the tour boats. For more information, call (206) 443-1244.

Celebrating a successful circuit around Blake Island.

The ride

Begin at Tillicum Village, several wood buildings just above the small Blake Island marina. Riding around the island counter-clockwise, find the trail below the buildings and bear right, following the shoreline. Just past Tillicum Village, the trail turns into a wide primitive road. At **.1 mile**, pass a trail on the left. At **.2 mile**, pass another trail off to the left. At **.4 mile**, stay on the main road. The road divides at **.6 mile**: take the right fork that drops down toward the water. At **1 mile**, when the road reconnects with the road from the previous fork, continue straight. At **1.1 miles**, the road forks: take the right fork down toward the water.

At **1.2 miles**, the road has dropped down from the banks of the island to beach level. At **1.25 miles**, reach a small campground on the northwest shore of Blake Island. At **1.3 miles**, turn up to the left, away from the beach. At bathrooms, **1.4 miles**, bear to the right, continuing up the hill. Find the road that continues around the perimeter of the island, well above the shoreline. **Whoa**, this is a difficult section because there are a number of roads in this area. At **1.6 miles**, the road divides; again take the right fork. You may have to walk up several short but steep hills along this stretch. At **1.7 miles**, the road forks: take the right fork. At **2 miles**, take the right fork.

After roller-coastering up and down, the Southworth ferry dock is visible at **2.5 miles**. Take a right at the fork, heading down. There is a beach access at **2.6 miles**. From the beach access, the road climbs steadily as you round the south end of the island. At **3.5 miles**, continue down the main road. Follow the main road into the camp area at **3.8 miles**. From here, follow the road around the field to the marina, **3.9 miles**.

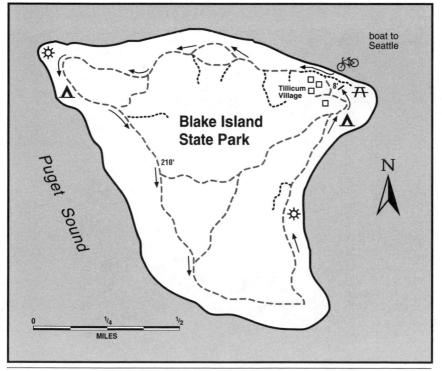

Ride 38 ✸ ✸ ✸ ✸

TAHUYA STATE FOREST

Checklist: 21.4 miles, Loop; dirt trails, dirt roads
Duration: 4–7 hours
Hill factor: endless rolling hills
Skill level: intermediate
Season: all year
Map: USGS Lake Wooten, Tahuya State Forest map
Ownership: public
User density: medium to high; motorcyclists, ATVers, bicyclists
Hazards: motorcycles at high speeds, getting lost

Prelude

Tahuya State Forest is a popular and extremely fun area to ride and explore. And exploration—call it forced exploration—is the operative word here since millions of trails exist and it's easy to get onto the wrong one. But if you pay attention, you should be able to get out before dark. The trail winds through light forests, roller-coasting up and down the entire way. Be aware that this entire forest is open to motorized vehicles.

To get there

From Bremerton, take Highway 304 west to Highway 3. Turn south onto Highway 3, and drive to the town of Belfair. From here, turn right onto Highway 300, the North Shore Road. Just past a store, turn right up the Belfair–Tahuya Road. After a short climb, find the Mission Creek Trailhead on the right.

Cruising down one of the many hills in Tahuya State Forest

The ride

From the Mission Creek Trailhead parking area, find the Overland Trail to the right; a sign points the way to the Mission Creek Trail. From the beginning, spur trails exit in every direction. Stay on the main trail by following the grey diamonds tacked to trees along the route and by using good sense. The trail is wide and muddy. At **1.4**

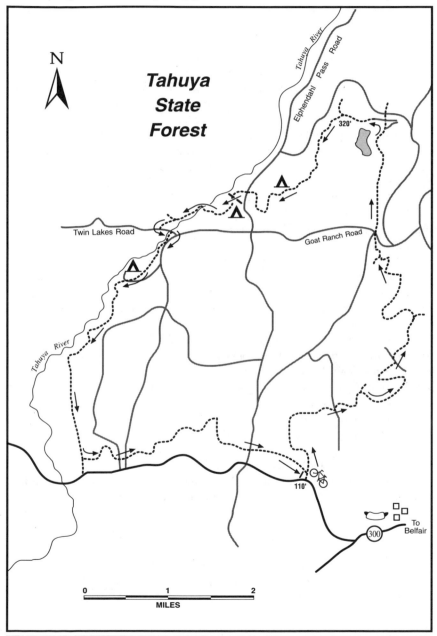

miles, the trail gets onto a dirt road by turning right and then jogs left back onto the trail. At **2.1 miles**, the trail forks. The left fork (straight) cuts several miles off this ride. Instead, take the right fork. The trail drops down to a bridge at **2.2 miles**, and then climbs steeply uphill to about **2.4 miles** where the road levels out as it bears to the right.

At **2.9 miles**, reach a road. Turn left and ride down the road following the arrows. About a hundred yards down the road, follow the arrow to a trail off to the right. At **3.4 miles**, the trail gets to a new dirt road. Take a right. Ride down the road to **3.6 miles** where the road forks. Go right; it quickly becomes the wide trail again. At **5 miles**, reach an intersection—take a left. The constant up and down takes its toll; a few steep pitches demand dismounts; spur trails exit off in every direction—watch for the grey diamonds.

At **7 miles**, reach an intersection—take the right fork which is basically straight. At **7.6 miles**, reach Goat Ranch Road, a wide two-lane gravel road. Directly across the road the trail continues. At **9.1 miles**, there's a lake on the left. At **9.3 miles**, reach a four-way intersection. Turn left toward Kay Canyon. At **9.4 miles**, take a left onto a road. Just down the road turn right, back onto the trail. At **9.6 miles**, take a left. At **11.5 miles**, reach a camp area and bear around to the left. At **11.8 miles**, veer to the right; the diamond markers are elusive.

Cross Elphendahl Pass Road at **11.9 miles**. **Whoa**, there are trails everywhere; watch for the diamonds to the left. At **12.2 miles**, keep following the markers. At **12.25 miles**, cross a paved road, and continue following the diamonds on the opposite side. At **12.5 miles**, pass by a camp on the left. Cross a road and then pass a camp area down to the right. Turn down to the right, pass the camp, and then cross the Tahuya River, **12.7 miles**. Bear to the left after the bridge. Parallel the Tahuya River for a short stretch. The trail reaches a road, then climbs a short hill before reaching a fork. Take the left fork, staying along the river. At **13.9 miles**, reach a road next to a large gravel area—Twin Lakes Road.

Turn left down Twin Lakes Road, and re-cross the Tahuya River. At **14 miles**, find a trail on the right that parallels the Tahuya River. Stay on the main trail; many spurs exit in all directions. The trail has been running parallel to a road. At **14.6 miles**, pass straight through a four-way intersection. At **14.75 miles**, pass the Tahuya River campground on the right.

The trail dumps out onto a road; turn right and ride to the hairpin turn in the road, where a trail exits left. This is the Tahuya River Trail, a muddy, winding, roller-coaster. After several miles the trail climbs away from the river. At **18 miles**, the trail bears left, parallel to a road. At **18.25 miles**, cross a dirt road. Continue straight along the trail. At **20 miles**, cross another dirt road. At **20.4 miles**, cross a paved road. At **20.6 miles**, the trail forks—take the right fork. At **21.4 miles**, arrive back at the Mission Creek Trailhead parking lot.

Ride 39 ⊛⊛

OLMSTED TRAIL

Checklist: 11 miles, Loop; paved roads, dirt trails
Duration: 1–3 hours
Hill factor: a steep paved climb up Interlaken, dirt downhills under I-5
Skill level: beginner
Season: all year
Map: City of Seattle
Ownership: City of Seattle, University of Washington
User density: heavy; cars, walkers, runners, dogs
Hazards: cars

Prelude

Although a beginning mountain biker can enjoy this ride, there is plenty of challenging riding to be found in the nooks and crannies around urban Seattle. Unfortunately, the Interlaken part of this ride was pared down by the Seattle Parks Department in late 1992, when the superintendant signed an order that banned bicycles from most trails in many Seattle parks (I'm glad I'm not a kid these days). Since Interlaken was developed by the Olmsted brothers—visionary planners who created many areas specifically with bicycle in mind—the closure was a significant slap. But the irony is especially caustic when you see the city's signs that designate Interlaken: a picture of a woman riding a fat-tire bicycle about 100 years ago, *on a dirt trail!*

Under Interstate 5 on the Olmsted Trail

To get there

Ride or drive to Green Lake in north Seattle. Park near the intersection of E. Greenlake Dr. N. and Ravenna Blvd. N.E.. You don't have to drive to Green Lake to begin, though, since you can pick up this ride anywhere along the way.

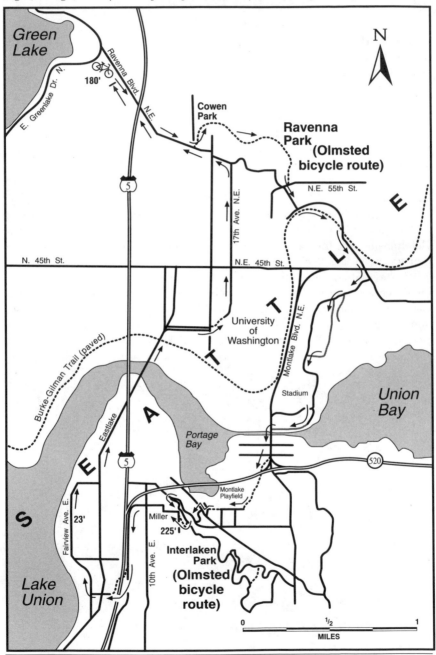

Balancing near Husky Stadium

The ride

From Green Lake, ride southeast on Ravenna. At **.9 mile**, Ravenna intersects Brooklyn Ave. N.E. at Cowen Park. Cross into Cowen Park, riding north, away from Ravenna. After several hundred yards the way slopes downhill, bears to the right, and passes under a high bridge. After the bridge, stay on the main path, a wide, gravel trail. Many walkers use this beautiful park, so keep the speed down. The trails on the slopes above the main trail through the park are off limits to mountain bicycles. Seattle Parks Department recently passed an order prohibiting mountain bicycles from trails less than five feet wide. At **1.7 miles**, after Cowan Park has become Ravenna Park, reach the baseball field. Ride around the edge of the field. Exit the park behind the backstop.

Emerge from the park on N.E. 55th Street; **1.8 miles**. Turn right and then immediately turn left down Ravenna Place N.E. Pedal for two blocks and find the Burke-Gilman Trail, **2 miles**. Turn left, immediately crossing 25th Ave. N.E., and continue on the Burke-Gilman. At **2.4 miles**, turn right off the Burke-Gilman Trail onto 30th Ave N.E. This street soon becomes Union Bay Place N.E. After several blocks, reach N.E. 45th Street, **2.6 miles**. Continue straight across the intersection, then take the first right, **2.7 miles**, onto Clark Road, toward the University of Washington playing fields, driving range, and parking areas. At **2.9 miles**, immediately past a tiny bridge and just before the driving range, turn left onto a gated, gravel road. Ride toward Husky Stadium with a narrow slough on your left. At **3.4 miles**, the gravel road bends to the right and ends at a paved parking area. Bear to the left, taking the road that winds around behind the stadium. Just behind the stadium, **3.6 miles**, ride past a large grassy mound on the left. Spend some time playing on it, but beware of the drains which are partially obscured by grass and can cause spectacular and stunning headers.

Just before the stadium parking lot, fork left, riding past the boathouse. Ride up the gravel road to Montlake Blvd. N.E., **4.2 miles**.

Turn left and, after crossing Montlake Bridge, ride south along the sidewalk. Just before the road passes over State Highway 520, **4.4 miles**, find a small cement path on the right that follows a fence. This path tucks under 520, winding around to the Montlake Playfield, **4.5 miles**. Follow the cement path along the field, turn right at the road—E. Calhoun Street. Stay on Calhoun for several blocks until it deadends at a short trail. After the trail, turn left onto 15th Ave. E., then immediately right onto Boyer. Take the first left, one block later, up 14th Ave. E., **4.9 miles**. At **5 miles**, turn right onto Delmar Dr. E. Take the first road on the left, E. Interlaken Blvd., **5.25 miles**.

Pedal up Interlaken to a wide trail that cuts up the bank to the right at **5.5 miles. Whoa**, easy to miss this one. (Parts of this short trail may be less than five feet wide, so technically you should walk your bicycle per Seattle Parks regulations.) After a short climb, reach a paved road, near the intersection of 13th Ave. E. and E. Miller Street, **5.6 miles**. Immediately turn left onto E. Miller Street. At 11th Ave. E., jog to the right and pick up Miller again; ride several blocks and pass through 10th Ave. E. Go straight through on Miller, continuing as the road bends left and parallels Interstate 5. At the bend Miller becomes Harvard Ave. E. At **6.3 miles**, Harvard reaches Lakeview Blvd. E. as it passes under I-5. Cross Lakeview and ride onto the dirt under the freeway, heading south. At **6.45 miles**, take the dirt alley down to the street below. Under the freeway: homelessness, garbage, Lake Union, Seattle Center, cement pillars.

From the dirt play area under the freeway, ride toward Lake Union on E. Blaine Street, across Eastlake, to Fairview Ave. E., **6.6 miles**. Turn right onto Fairview, then wind past houseboats. Turn right on E. Roanoke Street at **7.2 miles**. Turn left on Eastlake and pedal all the way to the University Bridge, and then up to E. Campus Pkwy. on the right. Take E. Campus Pkwy. to 15th Ave. E., turn left up the hill, then find a path to enter the University of Washington campus. Wind your way—your choice—through campus to the top at Memorial Way and N.E. 45th Street, **9.2 miles**. Cross through the intersection, continuing straight up what has become 17th Ave., reaching Ravenna Blvd. N.E. at **10 miles**. Turn left onto Ravenna, then ride two blocks down Ravenna to 15th Ave. N.E., where Ravenna is displaced slightly and 15th forces you to jog to the right before picking up Ravenna again. From here, take Ravenna all the way back to Green Lake, **11 miles**.

Ride 40 ✿

GREEN LAKE—LOWER WOODLAND PARK

Checklist: 4.3 miles, Loop; dirt and gravel trails
Duration: 1 hour
Hill factor: mostly flat, with rolling hills through Woodland Park
Skill level: beginner
Season: all year
Map: City of Seattle
Ownership: public
User density: high; runners, walkers, bicyclists
Hazards: cars

Prelude

Here's a short ride for the beginning rider who senses there might be something beyond the paved path around Green Lake. Despite the weekend throngs and the Lycra-sensibilities of the Green Lake culture, the trail around the lake and up into Woodland Park is fun, earthy, and usually not as crowded. Although this route is open to mountain bicycles, most trails in Lower Woodland Park are closed.

To get there

Pedal or drive to Green Lake, in north Seattle (near Exit 170 off Interstate 5). Travel south on E. Greenlake Way to N. 55th Street. Park in the lot next to the Lower Woodland Park playfields and track.

Photo by Peter Zilly

Cyclist pedaling around Green Lake

The ride

Beginning from the Lower Woodland Park playfields, ride south along the wide path that parallels Greenlake Way N. At N. 50th Street, turn right and ride up the hill. Pass some tennis courts on the right, then just before the tunnel, **.6 mile**, bear right into the gravel parking area. Ride catty-corner across the parking area to the grass. Ride up to the top of the grass hill, **.7 mile**. From here, ride north along the roller-coaster path that parallels Aurora Ave. N. From the top of the third hill, **.9 mile**, continue north on the trail (not the dirt road). Pass behind the bathrooms before reaching a paved parking lot. Ride through the parking lot, past the lawn bowling on the right. When you reach Whitman Pl. N. at the end of the parking lot, turn right. Immediately turn right again onto N. 63rd Street. Green Lake is now across W. Greenlake Way N. Cross the street and turn left on the dirt trail that circumnavigates the outside edge of Green Lake. At **1.3 miles**, the trail runs next to Aurora for about one-half mile. At **1.8 miles**, the trail bends away from Aurora. At **2 miles**, pass the Bathhouse Theater on the right. At **3 miles**, pass the Green Lake branch of the Seattle Public Library across Greenlake Dr. Pass Ravenna Blvd. at **3.2 miles** (see Olmsted Trail, page 133). At **4.2 miles**, pass the tiny, nine-hole golf course on your right. At **4.3 miles**, reach the intersection of E. Greenlake Dr. N. and W. Greenlake Dr. N. Cross W. Greenlake Dr. N. to the parking area and the end of the ride.

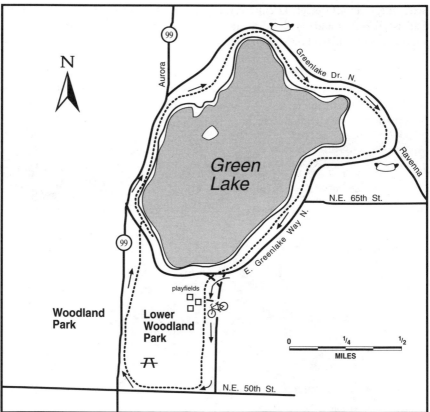

Ride 41 ✻✻

HAMLIN PARK

Checklist: 1.5 miles, Loop; dirt trails
Duration: 30 minutes
Hill factor: short hills throughout the entire loop
Skill level: intermediate
Season: all year
Maps: USGS Seattle North, USGS Edmonds East
Ownership: King County Parks
User density: high; runners, hikers, bicyclists
Hazards: falling in love with trees

Prelude
This is a great ride despite the short length. Most riders will do several loops, riding each successive loop with variations since there is a maze of trails. On sections of the trail, large Douglas firs garnished with salal belie the 1950s and 1960s subdivisions close by. Many people use Hamlin Park, so be courteous.

To get there
From Seattle, drive north on Interstate 5. Take Exit 175, N.E. 145th Street. Turn right (east) on 145th. Turn left on 15th Ave. N.E. Turn right at N.E. 160th Street. Drive .2 mile and park in the Hamlin Park parking lot.

Riding through snow at Hamlin Park

The ride

From the parking lot, ride out N.E. 160th back toward 15th Ave. N.E. After about 100 yards, find the dirt trail on the right. Pedal out the trail to a fork at **.2 mile**—stay on the main trail to the right. At **.3 mile**, reach another fork; this time turn left. Stay on the main trail to the cement barricades. Turn right at the barricades, and then quickly turn left before the second set of barricades. Ride straight on what seems like a trail, dropping to a field at **.45 mile**. Turn right at the field, continuing down a trail.

At **.5 mile**, pedal straight through a four-way intersection. About 100 yards farther, take a left, up and away from the main trail. At **.7 mile**, reach a fork: take a right, which switchbacks up the small ridge. At the top of the 50-yard hill, follow the main trail as it bears to the left, ignoring the three trails that spur off to the right. At **.8 mile**, take the right fork on the main trail. At **.9 mile**, reach a fork; take the lesser trail to the right, which descends vigorously for about 50 yards. Beginner riders may choose to walk this short section. At the bottom of the hill, turn right, away from the fence. When the trail comes to a fork at **1 mile**, take a right, walking up a short, rooted hill.

Whoa, at the top you'll discover a maze of trails. From the top, take the third left, **1.05 miles**, and then the first right. After a few more pedal strokes, **1.1 miles**, meet a trail and turn left, downhill. Stay on this main trail as it switchbacks once before reaching the bottom, **1.2 miles**. There is a very wide trail at the bottom, but instead of turning onto it, find the trail on the opposite side and begin climbing away from the wide trail. At **1.25 miles**, find a trail on the left and take it. At **1.35 miles**, the trail forks again: take the left fork. At **1.45 miles**, reach the paved road. Turn left and ride a short stretch down the hill to the parking lot, making the ride **1.5 miles**.

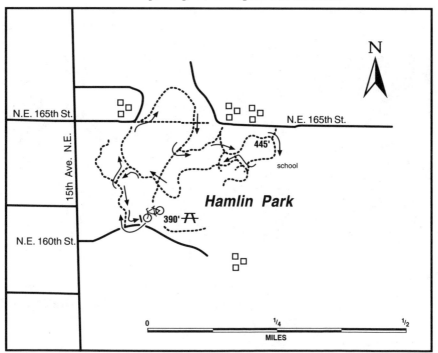

ABOUT THE AUTHOR

In 1980, high school diploma in hand, John Zilly spent nine months circling the United States on a bicycle, surviving 57 flats over more than 10,500 miles of riding. Several years later, after graduating from Whitman College in philosophy and touring by bicycle (more flats) through Europe, he put wide tires on his touring bike and set out to explore the trails of central Idaho. Those explorations developed into the **Mountain Bike Adventure Guide** and **Son of the Mountain Bike Adventure Guide**, both published by Adventure Press. In between writing books, working as a graphic artist, and playing on the slickrock in Moab, Zilly has published articles on cycling for numerous publications, including **Pacific**, **Northwest Cyclist**, **Sports Northwest**, **Southwest Cycling**, **The Times-News**, and **City Sports**.

NOTES

NOTES

NOTES